DO YOU BELIEVE IN GOD?

DO YOU BELIEVE
IN
GOD?

by

KARL RAHNER

Translated by

Richard Strachan

PAULIST PRESS

New York, N.Y.   Paramus, N. J.

Toronto

A Paulist Press edition, originally published under the title *Glaubst du an Gott?* by Ars Sacra Verlag, Munich.

NIHIL OBSTAT:
Anthony T. Padovano
Censor Librorum

IMPRIMATUR:
✠ Thomas A. Boland, S.T.D.
Archbishop of Newark

January 15, 1969

Library of Congress
Catalog Card Number: 70-77644

Published by Paulist Press
Editorial Office: 304 W. 58th St., N. Y., N. Y. 10019
Business Office: Paramus, New Jersey 07652

Printed and bound in the
United States of America

Contents

I

Can We Still Believe?

W E SPEAK of believing in the infinite mystery that we call God. We believe—try to believe—in this deepest of mysteries, which as *our* mystery has drawn near to us in Jesus Christ and his grace: a grace even when it is not recognized as such and where a man seems to be plunging into the black abyss of emptiness and nothingness.

Is it possible to profess this faith even today? It is not possible without dreading that one will fail to say the very thing which would have tipped the balance, giving a particular reader or hearer the courage to believe. All I can do is try to speak honestly.

The faith I am talking about is faith in the real sense of the word, faith that is rooted in personal decision, not simply in middle-class habit and the conventions of society. And therefore, nothing sound can be said about the future there is likely to be for faith unless one asks what influence faith has in our personal existence today. The future of faith will arise out of the personal decisions made by each one of us. Today we must answer for our existence.

Let me try to put the matter quite simply. I begin with the fact that I find myself a believer and have not

come upon any good reason for not believing. I was
baptized and brought up in the faith, and so the faith
that is my inheritance has also become the faith of my
own deliberate choice, a real, personal faith. God knows
that is how matters stand; his mystery sees into the depths
of my being, depths that are impenetrable to me. And at
all events I can say: "I have not come upon any good
reason to stop believing in God—to stop being the person
I am."

Before a man changes himself he ought to have good
reasons for doing so. If a man tried to change without
having such reasons, to give up this fulfillment of his
spiritual person, he would drop into the void; for him
there would be no escape from *disintegration*. A datum
must be accepted and upheld until it is disproved. One's
life and growth can spring only from a root that is already
alive, from one's own beginning, from the gift of primor-
dial trust in the meaningfulness of life.

When tradition has bestowed high and holy things on
a man and confronted him with an absolute summons,
then his critical conscience and probing reason may accept
this mere fact as sufficient evidence—both as unthematic
experience and as logical justification—for the truth of
the tradition. But whatever doubts may have assailed me,
one thing has always stood out in my mind, sustaining
me as I clung to it: the conviction that the experience
handed down to me must not yield to empty routine.
Spiritual dullness and benighted skepticism must yield
to nothing less than that mightier being who calls me into
a more remorseless light.

Of course the inherited faith was always a faith under
assault, but it was always experienced as the faith which
asked: "Will you also go away?" and to which one could
only say: "Lord, to whom shall we go?" (Jn. 6, 67f.) .

It was experienced as the faith that was mighty and kindly, that a man therefore would not have been justified in giving up unless, at least, its contrary had been proven true. But nobody has presented me with such proof, nor does it emerge from the experience of my own life.

Certainly there are many difficulties and many sources of bitterness in my mind and in my life. And yet it is plain that any difficulty which I am to entertain as a serious objection to my faith must correspond to the dignity and depth of what it would attack and alter. Intellectual difficulties may abound in the field of this science or that; they may arise from the history of religions, from biblical criticism, from the history of the early Church—difficulties to which I have no direct, pat answer. But these difficulties are too nice and too flimsy, compared with the gravity of existence, for me to let them decide ultimate issues and shape my whole life in its unutterable depths. For example, my faith does not depend on whether the right exegetical and Catholic interpretation of the first chapters of Genesis has been found or not, whether a decree of the Biblical Commission or the Congregation for the Doctrine of the Faith is eminently wise or not. Such arguments are ruled out from the start.

True, there are other and more profound trials. But when these are faced with honesty and courage, they bring out one's true Christianity for the first time. They affect the heart, the inmost core of existence. They place it in jeopardy and thrust it into the ultimate dubiousness of man—but precisely by so doing they may be the birth pangs of true Christian life.

Simply experiencing life isolates a man; it leaves him in a kind of void, exposed to his freedom and yet not assured of it; he finds himself lost in an unending sea of darkness, in a monstrous night where one only staggers from one makeshift to the next, frail, poverty-stricken, throbbing with the pain of finite existence, ever and again thrown back to one's dependence on the merely biological, on stupid institutions, on inherited ways (even when one resists them). A man feels death there inside him, in the midst of his life; he senses how death is the frontier that no one can cross of his own strength, how the ideals of life lose their youthful splendor and droop, how one wearies of clever talk at the annual fair of life and learning—yes, even learning.

The real argument against Christianity is the experience of life, this experience of darkness. And I have always observed that the elemental force and the arbitrary prejudgment which lie behind the technical arguments of the learned—or rather of individual learned men—against Christianity always spring from these ultimate experiences of existence which plunge mind and heart into darkness, fatigue and despair. These experiences seek utterance in the doubts of learned men—carefully as their doubts need to be weighed.

But the experience we are speaking of is also the argument *for* Christianity. For what does Christianity say? What does it preach? Despite an apparently complicated system of dogma and morals, it says something quite simple, nothing else but this: mystery always remains mystery, but this mystery wills to disclose itself as the infinite, the incomprehensible, the unutterable being that is called God, as intimacy that gives itself in an absolute self-communication in the midst of the experience of human emptiness. This intimacy has not only occurred in what we call grace; it has also become historically tangible in him whom we call the God-Man. Both these modes of divine self-communication—that of God "in himself" and that of God "for us"—involve what we call the threefold divine personality: three relations of God's one being and working: as the creator, as the sanctifier and as the inward guide and principle of unity.

Man finds it difficult to believe that this utter mystery is close to us and not remote, is love and not a spurning judgment. It is a light that may seem darker to us than our own darkness. But does it not bestow so much light, so much joy, so much love, so much glory in the world of faith as to cause us to say that all this can come only from an absolute light, an absolute love and glory, from an absolute being—even if we do not understand how this our darkness and nothingness can exist when infinite fullness exists, albeit as a mystery? Can I not say that I am right in clinging to light, be it ever so feeble, instead of darkness—to beatitude instead of the hellish torment of my existence?

Suppose I accepted the arguments which existence raises against Christianity. What would they offer me to live by? The courage of an honest man, perhaps—the nobility of one who resolutely faces an absurd existence? But then can this be accepted as something manly, binding and exalted unless again one has said that something honorable and glorious exists—and how can such a thing exist in the abyss of utter absurdity?

Now here we have said something significant. A man who boldly accepts life, even if he be a myopic positivist, has already accepted God as he is in himself, as what he wills to be for us in love and freedom, which means the God of eternal life in his divine self-communication. For anyone who really accepts *himself* accepts mystery as the infinite emptiness that man is and thereby tacitly accepts him who has decided to fill this emptiness that is the mystery of man with the infinite mystery that is God.

Christianity can be regarded as the clear affirmation

of what man obscurely experiences in his concrete existence. Man, after all, is not only superior to animals as a
spiritual nature; he is also a spirit inwardly alight with
love by God's grace. And if man, being such, really and
totally accepts *himself* as he is, mutely accepts himself in
this light, then that is faith, and Christianity is essentially
the affirmation in utter trust of this mystery, man, in the
spirit of Christ. If I acknowledge and affirm this fact,
what reason can I then have not to be a Christian? I
know of only one compelling reason: the weariness, sin
and despair that I experience in myself; the crumbling of
existence by a dreary skepticism which can no longer even
summon up a protest against existence; slothful evasion
of the unspoken but eternal question that we ourselves
are not facing or seeking to answer but from which we
are rather taking refuge in the wretchedness of daily
routine.

We would not deny that silent, patient uprightness in
attending to one's daily duties can also be a form of
"anonymous Christianity," a form in which many a man
(if he does not turn stubborn skepticism into an absolute
system) may be able to practice Christianity genuinely—
perhaps more genuinely than in certain more explicit
forms which are often lived so vacuously as a flight from
mystery instead of a real confrontation with it.

Experience of such anonymous Christianity, unex-
plicit but genuinely lived, might undermine one's Christian confidence that man is the finitude endowed with
God's infinitude. But if I should yield to this doubt, what
would I then have in exchange for Christianity? Emptiness, despair, night, death.

And what reason have I to regard *that* abyss as truer
than the abyss of God? It is easier to drop into one's own
emptiness than into the abyss of God's blessed mystery—

but it is not braver, and it is not wiser. Of course this truth only emerges if it is lived and accepted as "the truth that makes men free" and dares all things which lead us upward.

St. Augustine prays: "O God, the Father of truth . . . I call upon thee, wellspring, ground and author of the truth of all that is true" (*Soliloquies* I). I have called upon it and it attests itself to me and gives me what I must give it, so as to be and remain the blessed strength of life in me. It gives me the courage to believe in it and call upon it when dark night would swallow me up.

I see thousands upon thousands of men about me, whole cultures and eras that are explicitly non-Christian, and I see times coming when Christianity will no longer be taken for granted in Europe and the world at large. But when all is said and done, that cannot unsettle me. Why not? Because everywhere I see a Christianity that does not call itself Christian, because my explicit Christianity is not, for me, one opinion among others that gainsay it but the homecoming and flowering of what I can live elsewhere, too, as love and truth. I do not consider non-Christians to be people with less wit or less good will than I have. But were I to subside into a hollow, craven skepticism because there are many different views of the world, would I stand a better chance of reaching the truth than if I remained a Christian? No, for skepticism and agnosticism are themselves only opinions among other opinions, and the hollowest and most craven of opinions at that. This is no escape from the multitude of world views. Even refraining from any decision about them is a decision—the worst decision.

Besides, I have no reason at all to consider Christianity one world view among others. Let us understand exactly what Christianity is; let us listen carefully to what it really says and compare it, listen to its message with the utmost care but also with the utmost receptivity of mind and heart. Then we shall never hear anything good, true and redemptive illuminating our lives and opening up vistas of eternity that exists in another world view but is missing in Christianity. Elsewhere, indeed, we may hear things to rouse us, spur us on, widen our mind's horizon and enrich us. But all this is either something tentative which neither solves nor attempts to solve the ultimate problem of existence in the face of death—and then it can perfectly well be taken into the breadth of Christian living—or else it is something which we will recognize as a part of genuine Christianity if we but explore Christianity with more care, more courage and sharper eyes. Perhaps we shall observe that we never quite achieve a complete integration of this knowledge, these experiences, these realities of art, philosophy and poetry, with our Christianity as we have thought it out. But between any legitimate experience and knowledge on the one hand, and genuine Christianity on the other, we shall never discover any ultimate, irreconcilable contradiction. And that is enough.

Thus we have a right and duty to listen to Christianity as the *universal* message of truth which nothing can limit, and which rejects only the negations of other world views, but no real affirmation that they have to offer. Let us listen to Christianity as the universal message which embraces and thus preserves everything else, which forbids man nothing except to lock himself inside his finitude, except to disbelieve that he is endowed with God's infinitude and that as "finite he is receptive to the infinite."

Therefore we Christians do not look on non-Christians as people who have mistaken error for truth because they are more stupid, more wicked and more unfortunate than we, but as people who in the depths of their being are already pardoned, or can be pardoned, by God's infinite grace in virtue of his universal salvific will and are on the road toward perfection, as people who have simply not yet come to an explicit awareness of what they already are: men called by God. If we know this, it is a grace which we cannot yet attribute to those others; it is also a fearful responsibility weighing upon us, who now must be of our own accord what they are necessarily as men summoned by God. But the fact that others are only anonymous Christians is no reason for us not to be Christians explicitly.

We know full well that Jesus of Nazareth is *the* great sign that God himself has radically intervened in the world. This fact cannot be arrived at by logic; it is God's saving gift to mankind, no matter of course but an historical reality. It is not difficult to believe in Jesus Christ, the Son of God, on the basis of what he says of himself and the signs that mark his life and death. It is easy for a man who has been given love, which makes the hardest things easy.

For in the first place there is nothing mythological about this doctrine of the God-Man (the divine nature and the human nature, inseparable and unconfused in the one Person of the incarnate God). It is not mythology to say that in my mind's absolute transcendence (when my mind rises above immediate data) God's infinitude is given to me. And no more is it mythology to say that in one particular human being the transcendence of self (which otherwise is always a mere becoming) reached an absolute acme, because here God's self-communication to the created mind and spirit happened in a unique way. Now if one can really grasp *this* proposition in all its weight, one has affirmed God's incarnation as a *possible* embodiment of what it is to be man.

We must always bear in mind that, according to the Christian doctrine of the relation between the world and God, the more creatures belong to God the more independent they become; therefore, precisely because Jesus' humanity belongs to the eternal Word of God in the most radical way, he is man in the truest sense; he descended deepest of all into the abysses of human things and experienced the truest death of all. It does seem that people first arrived at the idea of the God-Man through God's actual incarnation. But once that event has taken place there is not much difficulty about identifying the biblical Jesus with it. Who but Jesus could give me the courage to believe such a thing? If, as Teilhard de Chardin says, there must be a point omega toward which all the history of man's world is headed, and if experience of my own grace-given closeness to God entitles me to expect that that acme really exists, then why must I feel sheepish about finding it in Jesus of Nazareth—in him who, even as he was dying, commended his soul into the Father's hands, in him who knew the mystery of man, the devouring judgment, death and abysmal guilt through and through and yet called the supreme mystery "my Father" and called us his "brethren"?

Argument will force no one to believe in Jesus of Nazareth as God's absolute presence. That faith is a voluntary thing, if only because its object is something historical, which therefore does not exist necessarily. But anyone who considers that ideas only become living truth in earnest when they stand forth in flesh and blood can more readily believe in the theandric idea if he believes in Jesus of Nazareth.

Something further must be said about the idea of the

God-Man and its embodiment in Jesus. Because he is God's assent to the world and the acceptance of the world into God, he is the eschatological event that will never be superseded. After him no prophet can appear who will displace him. For there are two words and things, each ordered to the other, which cannot be superseded: man as infinite questioning, and God as the absolute answer which necessarily remains mysterious because it is *God's* answer. That is why the God-Man cannot be superseded. Through him the world and history have found their own meaning—but not as though now the world could no longer have any history worthy to be enacted and pondered. Quite the contrary: now human history, which takes place in knowledge and freedom, has caught up with its true principle, can perceive its true destiny to be a *partaking* (2 Pet. 1, 4) in the God-Man Jesus Christ. And so with him history only begins on its proper level: the obscure and incalculable history of a mankind that knows it is hidden away in the love of God.

Human history, of course, still stands, as it has ever stood, in the sign of *conflict* between man and the mystery of God. But it may now be interpreted as the history of God's revealed love in spite of all the horrible things that have happened and are still to happen, perhaps even swelling to apocalyptic proportions. The meaning, the goal of history is the intimacy with God (an intimacy resting upon the God-Man) of all who are called and saved—an immediacy with God which by its nature is grounded and embodied in the God-Man Jesus Christ. From the very beginning we have been regarded as the brethren of the God-Man, so that it is possible to say with Soloviev that all mankind is truly theandric.

Now there is yet another hindrance and menace to faith: the very community of believers, *the Church*. To one who scans history with an unprejudiced eye, no doubt, she is holy Church, the sign raised among the nations; for as the fruitful mother of saints she bears witness that God is at work in her. But she is also the Church of sinners and to that extent a sinful Church, because we, the members of the Church, are sinners. This fact makes itself felt in what the Church herself does and refrains from doing. Sinful humanness, inadequacy, short-sightedness, falling short of what the hour demands, failure to understand the needs of the age, the tasks she assigns us and the direction in which she is heading—all these very human traits are also the traits of the Church's office-bearers and of all her members. It would be arrant self-delusion and a clerical arrogance ill becoming the Church as Jesus' community were one to deny or gloss over this sinfulness or pretend that it was rampant only in the Church of former ages. That sort of thing is an assault on faith which may practically suffocate the individual.

And yet, are we not ourselves part of this burden that weighs upon us and jeopardizes our faith? And if we know that truth can be fulfilled on earth, in the flesh, and not in a hollow idealism, if today we know better than ever that man can find himself only in a community which makes clear-cut demands, that any withdrawal of the individual into isolation is a fossilized ideal that was always wrong anyhow, then there can be only one course for the man of today: to put up with the burden of community as the one means to the freedom of the person.

And finally, we are baptized into the death of the Lord and receive his body, and we wish to be included in the community of saints. Now all that is possible only if we live in the Church and help bear her burden, which is also our own. The concrete Church may be a trial to our faith, but may also mature it, and need not be the cause of its death if we have not first let faith die in our own hearts.

Though it is no easy matter to judge one's own era, I do think that *young* minds have rather a hard time of it these days. It is especially difficult for them—and yet how necessary—to distinguish faith in Jesus Christ and his kingdom from matters on which opinions may differ widely. Society must be organized to a certain extent, but no clear-cut imperative as to world order can be deduced from the Christian message *alone;* this means that Christians, too, may hold different opinions about the dosage of order and freedom and therefore even about the suitability of man-made Church ordinances. Disagreement over such matters must be borne with sobriety and patience, in a spirit of love for the Church and the Church's people; a responsible attitude toward our own duties must be combined with obedience, longanimity and an ability to wait. A man who discharges his responsibilities toward the future by living this way in the Church will accept the Church's historical aspect and will not permit it to become a grave threat to his faith that God and Christ are present in the Church.

Here again it behooves us to have a sense of fraternal solidarity with those who do not outwardly belong to the Church. They are not free, either, to do whatever they choose; their road, too, has been marked out for them and they must keep to it in their concrete living—in their home life, in their career, in their social activities. To the extent that they make an effort to do so, they are *unconsciously* what the Christian is consciously and explicitly—and, Jesus would say, "not far from the kingdom of God" (Mk. 12, 34). Such a man may assume he is an atheist; he may grieve at the thought that he does not believe; concrete Christian doctrine may seem outlandish to him.

Let him but press on, following the light there in his heart of hearts, and he is on the right road; and the Christian has no fear that such a man will not reach the goal, even though he has not managed to turn his anonymous Christianity into explicit Christianity.

It is a Christian truth that a man who seeks has already been found by the One he is honestly looking for, albeit anonymously. All roads lead to him. "In him we live and move and have our being" (Acts 17, 28). Comprehending all things, he is comprehended by none. And therefore Christianity, faith in God through Christ in *one* Spirit, is child's play, because all it says is that we are called into the immediate mystery of God, waiting for the revelation of that which already is so—"that God [is] everything to everyone."

II

The Believer amid
Unbelievers

A CHRISTIAN's faith is not a purely private concern. We live in the community of faith which is called the Church, but in practice we are a "diaspora" everywhere today, sometimes even among our own relatives. I do not refer here to ecclesiastical divisions, to the fact that various Christian bodies are represented in our environment and even among our relatives; I mean that quite a number of people in our environment—let us face it—have in effect lost the faith, some of them becoming real enemies to the Church and officially leaving her.

If these were people who otherwise did not matter to us, with whom we had to have contact only in connection with our work or on the plane of civility, then the situation would be quite bearable. Or, rather, it would only be part of that depression of mind and heart which comes over us when we consider how little the name of Christ is known and loved in the world after two thousand years. But no! Often they are people who "belong" to us, whom we are attached to, who are bound to us by ties of blood, shared feelings, a common life and destiny, love—people dearer to us in many ways than those whom we call one with us in the "household of the faith."

What problems this situation brings in its train, what anxiety and grief! How must a mother's heart flinch as she wonders whether the faith or the unbelief in the world will win the hearts of her children! How mockery or contemptuous dismissal can wound when it comes from those we love! How many anguishing personal problems can arise, easy enough for the moral theologian to solve in theory but hopeless tangles in practice! What is a mother to say to her child when the father does not take part in the First Communion for which the child has been prepared in faith and love? What must she feel when every increase in the child's love for his father is a graver danger to the child's faith? Or what is a father to do when his daughter marries in disregard of the Church's law, so that he cannot recognize her marriage as valid before God? At what point does discretion become cowardice? At what point does confession of the faith become meddling? It is all too easy to become exasperated with Church authority, priests and fellow-Catholics because their behavior discredits Christianity in the eyes of one's non-Catholic relatives. One is angered by the mixture of faith and dubious opinions encountered in one's fellow Catholics. Instinctively one asks whether the science, art and noble humanity to be found outside Catholic circles are sufficiently in evidence inside them.

In any event, one cannot contrive to believe in the concrete Church without a thousand arguments, explanations and apologies (at least inwardly), because one always sees, as well, how things look to those "outside" whom one loves. But the darkest and most difficult thing about all this is the *question of the eternal salvation* of those we love. We hold that living by the faith which binds us to one another as members of the one mystical body is God's gracious and mandatory will, and it would be unloving on our part to pretend we have no duty of love to be concerned for the salvation of those with whom God's providence has connected us. Thus the burden of others weighs upon us. God's Word calls upon us to "work out our salvation with fear and trembling"—that is, in reverence toward the mystery of God. When a man so readily deceives himself and runs away from his ultimate responsibility, how could we fail to think of others' salvation in holy fear?

Here a few words on each of the two foregoing points must suffice.

First of all, we must closely acquaint ourselves with this state of neighborly togetherness between believers and unbelievers. Humanly speaking, no general change is to be expected in the sense of a return to living faith, even if we look no farther than our own immediate circle. More than ever before we shall be outsiders, even among those we love. Today the words of the Gospel about the discord which Christ brings into a man's very household (Mt. 10, 21f. 34ff.) , with the crisis of decision for him against one's own kin, have recovered their hard ring and practical significance.

But by God's will a fact is always a charge to us, a challenge and a grace. The faith of a man who has been marooned must be constantly won anew; he must live by his own resources and cannot be the sociological product of his environment. Faith will require more and more exertion against attacks without and troubles within. It will be a tree with less foliage and less blossoms than it used to bear, but it will have a deeper root and concentrate on essentials. It will be more personal in character and less institutional. But is such a faith, when lived, less genuine than the Christianity of the Middle Ages or of the baroque period? In those earlier days was it not also true

that one only became a true Christian when one started to
distinguish God's Word from the word of men, when one
obeyed the voice of conscience though all the world was
of another opinion?

Today a Christian's faith is more personal, less influ-
enced by environment than in past centuries. Therefore
it stands in greater jeopardy. Frail man has no business to
be idly conjuring up dangers. But where dangers exist, he
has the promise that God will be faithful.

In the second place, burdensome though the present
state of diaspora may be for the Christian, it is also a
grace and he must not evade it by remaining aloof as far
as possible from his relatives and his fellow men. One
could live in semi-isolation nowadays, for, after all, one
earns one's own bread and butter. But it should not be
done. There may be extreme cases where danger and
enmity are such that a man is left no choice but to go
forth like Abraham from his kindred and the house of
his fathers (Gen. 12, 1). Generally speaking, however, we
should beware lest faith become a pretext for denying our
parents, relations, and fellow men what we owe them by
God's will and even by nature (Mk. 7, 9-13). The Christian's very responsibility for himself means that he must
be more independent in his thoughts and feelings than
the average man is, but this attitude should not be ex-
tended to matters where it is unsuitable.

Paul thinks that a marriage should continue (insofar
as it depends on the Christian party) if one of the partners
embraces Christianity, and that judgment has a bearing
on our problem. The apostle expects the marriage to be a
blessing for the relatives, even though they are not, or
not yet, Christians (1 Cor. 7, 14). Being loyal in this way,
both to God by faith and to fellow men who think differ-
ently, may wring one's own heart; yet the thing must be

borne. A heart that loves bravely and selflessly will find the right road—laboriously perhaps and having to try again and again—but in this world we are not called to do more than work at a task which is never completed.

And in the third place a modest word shall be said about the most obscure point in our whole subject: concern for the eternal salvation of our friends and relatives who do not share our faith. We Catholics today tend to give the impression that we are embarrassed by the subject and steer clear of it; on the one hand we discourse upon the Church as the necessary means to salvation, and on the other we evade a whole cluster of problems in real life— that is, when the doctrine becomes concrete.

One thing, of course, is obvious: we have no real, definite answer in the case of any individual—not in the case of anyone, not even of "good Catholics" who die fortified by all the holy sacraments. On the gravestones of those who died believers, in communion with the Church, we write: "May they rest in peace"; we write these words because they express the hope we are bidden to cherish for ourselves and for others. But the hope does not anticipate God's judgment. All men, good believing Christians like the rest, pass without a word into the darkness of God, and no one knows what judgment he pronounces. Even the earthly Jesus said that he judged no man (Jn. 8, 15). But this uncertainty for all our fellow men may be embraced by hope for all.

The fact that a man—so far as we can observe—has died in the peace of the visible Church is one more reason to hope for his eternal rest, one more reason for hope which we do not have for others. We ought to accept this difference in mute humility. "Who are you, a man, to answer back to God?" (Rom. 9, 20). But we may and indeed must hope that all other men will receive God's saving mercy.

First of all there is the quite universal validity of what Pius IX said over a hundred years ago: "We must firmly hold that no one who lives in invincible ignorance of the true religion incurs this guilt [of not adhering to the faith of the Church] in the eyes of the Lord. And who will presume to think he can identify the cases where such ignorance is no longer possible? How very disparate such cases can be according to the character and variety of peoples and countries and the dispositions of the individual" (Denz. 1647).

This must not only be said of distant pagan nations and bygone ages; it applies equally to people *living in our midst*. Scripture and the Church teach that every human being is given sufficient grace to work out his salvation. Therefore, every human being who has reached the point where he is able to make moral decisions can forfeit salvation only through his own fault, and every human being who finds his salvation finds it on the road which logically leads to the visible Church. But it does not follow that *every* individual must be given a sufficient grace capable of flowering into visible membership of the Church during his lifetime. To affirm that it does would amount to saying that every adult who has lived for a considerable time among Catholic Christians without becoming a Catholic has committed the grave sin of rejecting the grace offered to him. Such an allegation not only cannot be proved, but it also offends against love and against the respect that we owe to the decisions of other people's conscience—so long as their guilt has not been positively demonstrated (and we will hardly undertake to demonstrate it).

There is divine grace, through Christ, for the "many"

(Mt. 20, 28; cf. 1 Tim. 2, 6)—that is, for all who stand before him, from the first man to the last—and therefore there is divine grace in Christ outside the visible Church as well. It would be an error to suppose that acceptance of grace can in every case·explicitly develop into the mature form of Christian faith. Thus it may happen that a man has submitted to God through faith, somewhere in the depths of his conscience inaccessible to us, without this salvific process having flowered into full Catholic Christianity.

Theologians inquire what is necessarily involved in this pardoning at the bottom of the heart. The conditions which they lay down (generally with an eye to Hebrews 11, 6: "Whoever would draw near to God must believe that he exists and that he rewards those who seek him") are such that many people "outside" can fulfill them—the more so since the Church teaches that every genuine moral decision entails at least an unconscious acknowledgment of God. And there is the Catholic theological opinion, at which no one demurs, that a man is given the grace necessary for salvation even when he is reverently disposed to believe, although he never hears of Christ's Gospel. We read in the Letter to the Romans: "When Gentiles who have not the law do by nature what the law requires, they are a law to themselves, even though they do not have the law. They show that what the law requires is written on their hearts, while their conscience also bears witness and their conflicting thoughts accuse or perhaps excuse them on that day when, according to my gospel, God judges the secrets of men by Christ Jesus" (Rom. 2, 14-16).

If we think this over, we shall not look on the virtues of pagans as "glittering vices" or assume that they are mere natural goodness, forerunners of salvation in Christ. Rather we will be quite ready to take it that these virtues are sustained by Christ's grace and produce eternal life. Nor can it be said that this only happens with a man in whose consciousness there is some explicit knowledge of Christ's grace. Thus when we meet people in our environment whose moral conduct compels respect, they may be people in whom the power of God in Christ is already at work without their being aware of the fact. I say they "may" be, but that is grounds enough for a confident hope on our part. For we really do not know anything *more* about ourselves and yet we confidently hope.

Here a word is in order about the Scholastic maxim: "Good requires causality whole and entire; evil results from any lack." This maxim is often understood in too simple and harsh a sense. In principle it is true that a man may forfeit salvation by offending God in *one* respect even though there is something to be said for his life, religiously and morally, in other respects. But then is there no truth to the ancient idea (which helped to shape the theology of the Fathers themselves) that a man's good and evil works are weighed against each other in a balance? In the living of his life, is a man really so made that one bit of him can be quite sound while the other is quite rotten, the whole of him thereby becoming rotten and incurring the doom of a reprobate? It is surely more correct to say that a man is stamped by the whole of his nature and freely disposes of himself (though he may not manage to do so every single moment). If this is true, then we may cherish a hope; when we meet a man who impresses us as having made his decision for the good on some point concerning the moral order, in such a way that good somehow stamps his *whole* being, then we have good grounds to hope that those of his attitudes which cannot yet be judged correct by the standard of Christian faith at least do not spring, subjectively, from that inmost core of his being whence alone any subjectively grave sin can spring.

Now how do matters stand with those individuals in particular, closely connected with us or not, who were once Catholics but no longer are and no longer wish to be? Does the Letter to the Hebrews not pronounce these remorseless and terrifying words: "It is impossible to restore again to repentance those who have once been enlightened, who have tasted the heavenly gift, and have become partakers of the Holy Spirit, and have tasted the goodness of the Word of God and the powers of the age to come, if they then commit apostasy" (Heb. 6, 4-6)?

Let only two things be said for the consolation of those who rightly grieve over someone dear to them who was once a Christian and has lost the faith, although we realize that this consolation will not banish all anxiety or lessen the responsibility to do everything possible for the return of the wanderer. The question is simply whether there may not still be room for hope even in such cases.

First of all, when Vatican Council I says that Catholics who have once embraced the faith of the Church can have no good reason for abandoning it or doubting it (Denz. 1794; cf. 1815), the case meant, as in the text of Hebrews which we have quoted, is that of a man who has consciously accepted the faith and then given it up—which is not necessarily the case of every individual who was once a Catholic and now is one no longer. Even where a young person is comparatively fervent, his Christian attitude may be something he has largely absorbed from his environment, only a preliminary to that personal decision to believe which our texts have in mind. Thus it may happen that an individual's religious growth never, in fact, gets beyond the preliminary stage where it is a reflection of the environment, never reaches that personal maturity which alone can make it a grave sin to abandon the faith. Cases of this kind are bound to be more common nowadays than they once were; for young people today, even when they grow up in a Christian home, encounter so many obstacles to their religious growth and are exposed to so many anti-religious influences that it often seems doubtful whether their Christianity has really attained the depth of personal conviction which must be involved before apostasy becomes a grave sin.

But let us assume that a person *has* lost the faith through serious sin. And let us also assume that this person is now of full age or getting on in years. May we say that his sin against faith can only be repented of and blotted out if he once more accepts faith in the same form in which he abandoned it earlier? No such thing can be proved. Rather, we can think of cases where a return to the faith which the person once practiced is impossible and yet a conversion to God occurs.

Psychological reasons chiefly account for these cases. Every free decision, whether good or sinful, creates habits of mind, trains of association, patterns of behavior, emotional involvements and mental blind spots which are connected with that decision and yet distinct from it and can therefore continue in being even if the free decision has ceased to exist in its primitive kernel because of a contrary decision.

Another point must also be taken into consideration. Theologians teach that there is such a thing as implicit repentance, one where a man does not look directly at his past action as such and repudiate it, but, without expressly recognizing his defection as sinful, so definitely affirms moral good that the real marrow of his former attitude is thereby given up and repudiated. How much we morally mature, how much moral wisdom we learn in this way as the years go by! And so, in view of all this it is not inconceivable that a man could part company, in the depths of his conscience, with his former sin (supposing he has really abandoned the faith) and recover the genuine attitude of a believer even though he be unable to get over the mountain of prejudice against ecclesiastical Christianity which he has accumulated.

While turning over these thoughts in our mind, we must not forget one thing: what God's revelation tells us about men's prospects of salvation is chiefly what we ourselves need to know, not all that falls within God's field of vision. Our business is to work out our salvation, and we are called upon to do everything possible so that God's salvation shall palpably have its own way even on earth, in us and in others. Therefore, the ways of mercy that are known to God remain shrouded in darkness for us. We are told what *we* must do. "Once we are freed from the trammels of this bodiliness and see God as he is, then we shall perceive for the first time how closely and harmoniously God's mercy and his justice are bound together" (Pius IX).

Nevertheless, even though we have grounds for hope, that is no excuse for standing idle. How could we be so apathetic as to neglect explaining the faith to those we love? The Church and we individual believers have a mission to others, because without us they may be lost, and also because God wills the grace and truth of Christ to be a "sign" for the world. It is not only for the salvation of the individual that the Church's Word and sacrament matter; everyone shares in the mission to the "many" as best he can, and a man who places himself at the service of this mission is entitled to hope that God's mercy is at work even in places that we do not reach. He is also entitled to hold his tongue when saying anything would be pointless.

He may trust that prayer, good example and patiently putting up with the diaspora, even in our own family, is a meaningful form of pastoral work, one no less important than direct action.

It would be perverse to suppose that we can be certain of all men's salvation. We must work out our salvation "in fear and trembling" (Phil. 2, 12)—that is, in reverent humility—and allow God to have his secrets. But if we thus forego trying to guess what is to be, we are also called upon to hope, even "believing in hope against hope" (Rom. 4, 18). "God is greater than our hearts, and he knows everything." He has set us in an age when there are Christians everywhere, certainly, but living in a diaspora. That is bound to be so if Christ must remain "a sign that is spoken against" (Lk. 2, 34) unto the end, and the Apocalypse depicts the war of unbelief against faith as even fiercer toward the end. We are called upon to bear these things with a responsible Christian mind, and we may hope for the salvation of all men because our impotence does not set limits to God's mercy.

III

Intellectual Honesty
and Faith

I F WE are asked whether the attitudes named in the title of this chapter are compatible, the answer depends on what is meant by "intellectual honesty." If it can be said that an honest man does not delude himself about anything, that he frankly faces the difficulties involved in taking up a philosophical position, that he is quite prepared to credit the defender of a different viewpoint with as much intelligence and good will as himself, that he is able on occasion to change his opinion and tries to be objective, modest and reasonable, that he allows for the fact that he himself is not free of prejudices induced by the spirit of the times, by his social background, by his schooling and profession, even by his own interest—then he has been described in such a way that we can readily accept the two attitudes of intellectual honesty and faith as compatible.

Intellectual honesty stands poles apart from the attitude of one who shirks personal decision about religion and, reversing the biblical admonition: "Test everything; hold fast to what is good; abstain from every form of evil" (1 Thess. 5, 21f.), tests everything but holds nothing fast

and withdraws still undecided. Of course, if a man honestly thinks he can do no better than be a worried atheist
—"tone-deaf in religious matters," as one individual said
who had no criticism at all to offer of his Christian kins-
folk—then he can accept that as his personal fate and
Christians have no business saying he has committed the
sin of unbelief. But it would be unsound to claim that
one's own indecision is the only attitude that intellectual
honesty can allow a man to take. How can anyone know
such a thing? How can anyone know that it is wholly
impossible to believe despite intellectual difficulties?

At any rate we are "doomed" to *freedom*—or blessed
with it. And this freedom is operative even in our ultimate
spiritual decisions. No ultimate, basic attitude, Christian
or non-Christian, can be arrived at without the strenuous,
bold decision of a free man—not because here blind im-
pulse calls the tune but because here insight and freedom
of action cannot be divorced. And therefore a man who
refuses to commit himself for fear of following an insight
that cannot be mathematically verified does *not* in fact
remain free but rather enters upon the worst of all com-
mitments—that of living his life without commitment. He
tries to live as a neutral, deciding nothing, and that in
itself is a decision, one for which the grounds are not
patently better than the grounds for any other decision.

Thus there is no doorstep to decision on which one can
just stand. Attempting to remain undecided simply means
refusing to face the issues of life consciously. In practical
living, decisions *are* made all the same, and it is only
logical, therefore, to ask whether one finds life absurd or
full of unutterably mysterious meaning. In short, intellectual honesty demands the courage to make a spiritual
decision, even if this decision is fraught with all the uncertainty, enigma and hazard that mark freedom itself

and that are inseparable from the spiritual decision of finite man as history has molded him.

A believer is well aware what reverence he must show toward the mystery of God in man. No one can judge how far another man may have gone along his road without yet deciding against the sacred meaning of existence. And so this decision of one who seems not to respond (speaking purely in the abstract, for God alone sees into a man's heart) may nevertheless affirm what the believer experiences as the blessed mystery of existence, whereas his inquiring partner in dialogue has not yet been given courage to tell himself outright the thing that the living of his life tacitly confesses.

A second misunderstanding about the bearing of intellectual honesty on faith is the idea that in order for a man to believe and yet remain intellectually honest he must have "scientifically" thought out every conceivable implication of faith—every implication of belief in God and belief in Christ, of redemptive history and of the Church in its every aspect. Were this really the case, then intellectual honesty and faith would in effect be locked in hopeless conflict. For who could make bold to say he was even capable of such a feat during the short span of his life, given the duties that are assigned to him, his limited opportunities for acquiring expert knowledge and his amateur standing in many fields? There is no need for us to draw up a full list of the disciplines involved. Who could think through every last item? Even in his own field, a theologian of our day finds himself on the same footing as any other Christian believer when it comes to intellectually justifying his personal faith. Since such is the case, is it only possible in the abstract for a believer to be intellectually honest?

No doubt there are interpretations of religion (non-

Catholic ones) which simply eliminate straight thinking
from faith, treating faith as a wholly irrational experience
that has nothing to do with intellectual honesty. Such an
idea of faith is far from the Catholic idea where an intellectual element is essential. Moreover, faith, as Catholics
understand it, concerns historical realities which do not
automatically lie beyond the reach of rational inquiry.
An altogether irrational faith can only arise in dreamers
and fanatics.

Faith must be able to justify itself before what one
conscientiously regards as intellectual truth. But that does
not mean that every single Christian must be versed in
fundamental theology so that his learned arguments may
adequately justify his attitude. For the intellectual life of
man is always and necessarily such that he absorbs lessons
from mere living which are not of a learned nature and
which the individual can neither work out nor check for
himself. Therefore, a man's sense of truth gives him the
right and duty to allow for the difference there is between
actual living and the knowledge that one takes over, by the
nature of things, from society as a sort of interest-free loan
without being able to test it all beforehand. A mature
person will understand that this difference cannot be set
aside. He knows that his living cannot be guided exclu-
sively by what he has thought out for himself, and that
he is therefore obliged to accept this difference and undertake an absolute commitment in the living of his life—
a religious commitment, that is—to commit himself *before*
he has scientifically examined all the implications. Were
he to refuse, then logically he would have to go back to
the beginning of his existence.

This does not mean, of course, that intellectual scrutiny and discrimination have no place in life and are never
incumbent on man. A certain area of reflection and

critical examination is part of human existence. The practical answer supplied by living keeps tossing to man an unanswered question that he must ask himself, but a man would be irresponsibly scrupulous, rather than intellectually honest, if he supposed that every single component of intellectual life must be scientifically examined before it is put to use. Where would that end? In order for any grown-up son to practice filial love toward his parents, must he first study the documents relating to the matter ånd ask his conscience questions under oath? Before adopting a political attitude must one first minutely examine the objective correctness of one's impressions and experiences? And would skeptical neutrality not be a decision as filled with consequences as a forthright decision for or against? Everyday living exacts decisions of us, and skeptical abstention, too, is a decision, although not the most courageous of decisions.

In our heart of hearts we are called on to make the decision of faith before the absolute, imperious mystery of existence, before God. Here a man of intellectual honesty has to consider the whole meaning of existence in general. Christian faith confronts us with decisions in every sphere of human life. Here the gulf between what is meant and the grounds for it, on the one hand, and what abstract scientific thought has worked out, on the other, yawns widest. However, there is no need for the man of intellectual honesty to be alarmed. Many particular problems are involved in a completely rational justification of faith (of the surrender which is faith) that an individual cannot directly solve on a scientific basis. But then intellectual honesty does not require that of him. Why should one not ingenuously trust to one's experience of life here, as one does in other matters, even if it is not yet worked out in theory—and never will be altogether? Take the case of love, for example, a trusting decision filled with consequences and yet one that has not been "scientifically thought through."

As an activity of intellectual life which embraces the ultimate meaning of existence, faith exhibits that absolute, unconditional character which it must have in order to be faith. But for that purpose no complete theological exposé of all its implications is necessary in addition to God's inner light. Faith primarily justifies itself by the light and strength it brings into people's lives. That light and strength represent a fact in which, as a rational being, one can rightly have confidence, especially as the contrary does not carry conviction. Faith gives life an order and a meaning; it opens up that infinitude which alone can bring life into harmony by its sway. And our conscientious sense of truth bids us cleave to that meaning of life, at the very least, until we learn of a still nobler, purer, fuller one. Faith feels that it is sustained and embraced by God's grace and thus finds itself attested to in its very act of surrender to mystery.

The demands of intellectual honesty are fully satisfied if the experience of faith, in a particular Christian, does not clash with his rational knowledge. Faith at large contains a critical element. Critical reflection, the effort to see what intellectual justification there is for faith, will and must take time. It is most apt to start with those problems which life presents to each individual in his particular circumstances. And a man with a genuine critical attitude (a gift of wisdom) will refrain from entering into many questions which theoretically arise but which have no necessary relevance for him as a concrete individual. Many matters he will duly recognize as beyond his competence.

As to the mystery of God in Christian life, God is the

incomprehensible, impenetrable mystery which the Christian confesses. Christianity is not a religion that includes "God" as a known quantity in the reckoning of human existence so that the answer will come out even. Rather, it is religion that sets man in the incomprehensibility which embraces and pervades his existence and will not let him imagine that some intellectual construction is a magic formula for understanding and mastering the whole of existence, which would be believing in an idol. God is and always will be unutterable mystery. All we know of God is what we learn by adoring mystery. We can draw near to him only by humility—that is, by the authenticity of our human existence.

A believing Christian has no idea of meeting with God as though he were an individual being within the sphere of existence. Rather, he deals with God as with that which incomprehensibly and unutterably sustains us, which interpellates us by the very fact of enabling us to go in quest of it, the source and ground of our quest. Christian faith insists that we must not slight this blinding darkness which embraces our life and pervades all things, the mystery of God; we must not evade this awesome being but must stand firm in its presence.

There is more. At the moment it does not matter whether a man makes bold to perceive this actual truth by the inward experience of his pardoned conscience, or whether he has the impression that it is the quintessential theme running through the religious history of mankind, where God's grace works in secret too, after all, or whether he receives the message straight from the witness of Christ and his apostles. In any case the reality of God is part of the genuine message of Christianity and means this: the mystery of our existence, which embraces us and which we call God, does not wish to remain the mere remote horizon tacitly enveloping and guiding our existence, but gives itself to us in a real self-communication so that we shall be partakers of its divine life. God himself is the grace of our existence.

Accordingly what we call creation—all those things that are not God and have been freely brought into being by the divine *operatio ad extra*—turns out to be the mere scene set for God's self-communication, bestowed on his "image and likeness" with the gratuitous love he himself is. God creates because he wills to communicate himself to us. For him, expressing himself is parting with himself; distance exists so that there may be union in love; covenant and law go before so that this union may come about, obedience to God so that we may enjoy God's freedom, experience of God's remoteness so that there may be the miracle of his forgiving intimacy. We do not say all this to clear up the mystery, but so that the mystery itself may be a joy to the heart.

However, is such a statement really *credible?* First, we must certainly say that such a complex of statements, which always convey the totality and oneness of human existence, is bound to present the mind with the utmost difficulty, if only on linguistic grounds. By the nature of the case there are no fixed, unequivocal terms to describe that totality. Precisely because we are dealing here with the absolute truth of man as the primal, indefinable mystery, what we say is bound to be obscure. The dangers inherent in this linguistic state of affairs disappear, however, when we also find that all these religious statements, be their terminology what it may, convey a mystery neither thought out nor conceived of, and that it is their nature to point out mystery. A man who reads them in this sense ceases to fear that nothing at all is known for certain, for all the affirmations of faith refer us to the one abiding mystery that must abide.

If intellectual honesty commands us (not forbids us) not to equate the fullness of reality and truth with the sum of the realities and truths which are known and obvious to us, if mystery then is not a marginal phenomenon of intellectual life but rather its abiding principle— what sort of intellectual honesty shall forbid us to believe in the experience of grace and the message of revelation which clarifies that experience, or to believe that this holy mystery wills to bestow itself on us as our inmost and loftiest life by a pardoning, divinizing self-communication? I cannot see that there is any objection to accepting this —the heart of Christian faith. A man needs the utmost grace-given courage in order to accept this faith, since it promises the unimaginably noble thing which alone really makes man far more than a clever animal. Have we not a duty to let God be greater than our stingy heart—and so to believe that God can reach our door and we his?

IV

Is Faith Possible in Today's World Picture?

MAN HAS entered upon a really creative stage of his historical evolution in which he is the logical planner and ingenious maker of things. This fact is clear in the religious domain as well.

Man always lives in an environment; he has always had and always will have dealings with something outside himself on which he depends. Formerly it was nature which sustained him and to which he felt a closeness. Nature to him was the majestic and mighty ruler, invested with the fearful yet magnetic splendor of the numinous, the mysterious, the exalted, who nurtured and cherished, was angry and destroyed, a law unto itself. This meant that God's dominion and the dominion of nature were experienced as very much the same thing. God spoke in nature; his favor and his wrath made themselves felt along with nature and through it. Storms, pestilence, thunder-bolts, a new spring bursting forth, earthquakes—these and a thousand other events, being uncontrollable and un-foreseeable in their coming and going, seemed to give man a direct experience of God's dealings with him. Thus within the framework of open, uncontrollable nature, the history of nature and the history of God's salvation and damnation seemed to be one or else to merge imperceptibly into each other.

It was the same in the Old Testament, although not to the extent that Israel deified nature or confused nature with God. It recognized the sun, moon, stars and powers of this earth as God's creation and did not take them for manifestations of God. But nature was regarded as God's viceroy, and therefore man had no alternative but to obey in mute humility or invoke and beseech the sovereign ("pantocratic") Lord of nature.

Today the case is vastly different. Whether this change is called one of kind or one of degree only depends on the aspect in which one views the change. The change is closely bound up with modern natural science (and in addition with the conversion of philosophy to the subject at the beginning of modern times), and there is more to it than Christian minds generally appreciate. It will make further enormous strides in the technological age we are just entering, thanks to automation and cybernetics, and alter men's outlook still more.

Even today, of course, wild uncontrollable nature does exist, but to the mind of contemporary man it is little more than a survival, an island of popular tradition left over from earlier days. I do not say this is actually true, but this is the general feeling about it.

The change is tremendous. No doubt, storms still occur which we fail to control, but in our industrialized countries we no longer starve if the harvest in a certain area is destroyed by storms. We still become sick, but we know what our illnesses are and how to combat them, and we have at least doubled man's expectation of life. We no longer live *in* nature; we transform it. We are no longer thinking subjects who pit themselves intellectually and religiously against stubborn nature and feel more than its equal because of a direct relationship with the divine Lord of nature; even in daily life this nature has become the material and tool of man's creative activity.

In wide areas we do not face a nature that God has made but the one we ourselves have made: *our* light, *our* new fabrics, means of transportation *we* have invented, plants and animals *we* have grown or bred. And today these things are no longer lucky accidents or hazardous ventures but the results of rational planning which sets its goal and then ordains that the goal must be reached by a particular means. Enthusiastic reports and descriptions of space travel may depict a future that is more or less a dream and perhaps unattainable. But one still shudders to think that a man-made sphere can be fired from earth onto the moon which God set in his heaven to illuminate the night, whereas formerly—even in the Old Testament world picture—the moon belonged to a realm whose inhabitants were proof against all the ravages of time.

In short, to modern man nature is no longer the high viceroy of God, set beyond his control, but the material he needs to experience himself in his own free creativity, to build his own world for himself in accordance with his own law. Doubtless this material with which man works still has laws proper to itself which continue to weigh heavily upon him; doubtless man's creativity remains inexorably subject to what is antecedently there, and is not pure creativity such as we acknowledge in God; doubtless its growth is always a growth of obedience and servitude to an alien law—but it is a conscious and deliberate creativity which masters nature and thrusts it into man's own service.

Thus in a real sense, not a merely spiritual one, man is left in his own hands, and to that extent the world which surrounds him is very largely his own image.

We do not deny that individuals experience this transformation in vastly different degrees, according to their profession, age, immediate environment and culture, and the courage with which they accept this experience or repress it. Let us admit that the clerical world (which exists in all religions), because of the threat to spiritual life, is slowest and most loath to undergo this experience. But on the whole it is increasingly true, of necessity, that the man of today and tomorrow has become a real subject, has gained a tremendous amount of control not only in the abstract but in practice, and puts the change into effect not only intellectually and religiously but also practically, in direct contact with a science which does not contemplate the beauty of the world but considers how nature can be conquered and crushed, have the laws of its behavior wrested from it, and become man's own. There is a danger that the art of "leadership," of advertising and propaganda, may induce man to regard even human beings as so much material to be molded in light of his own interests and self-appointed ends, in *his* world where he finds himself very nearly his own creator and God.

Before we inquire further into the significance of this process for man's relationship with God, another observation must be made as regards intellectual history and theology: this evolution is *inevitable,* and ultimately fits in with the nature of Christianity. All romantic yearnings for pure nature, its noble, divine sway, its unspoiled beauty and fruitfulness, are and remain romanticism. Even where we spare nature, where we set up national parks and green belts, keep rivers free of sewage and try to prevent the extinction of the whale, the nature which survives in this way is still that which *we* have voluntarily refrained from destroying; it is the nature we have arranged, our garden, and therefore not the nature which the ancients lived in as an integral part but the nature we have made, artificial nature, a nature which is a refinement of civilization and reflects the image of man.

This evolution is inevitable. Marxist ideology need not be brought in to explain it, nor need one consider it a triumph and a blessing, but it is here to stay. What matters a great deal more is that if we really scrutinize intellectual history and the nature of Christianity, we shall find that this evolution has not happened despite or against or alongside Christianity but arises from the very nature of Christianity and forms part of its history. The fact that this connection can only be discovered once the new phase of history is under way, that we have often lived through this phase in a state of alarm, unwilling to understand it, does not alter the reality. We are concerned with the history of our own religion, with a phase of Christianity. For nowhere is man *more* God's free partner than in Christianity; so true is this that he does not undergo his eternal salvation but must *make* it in freedom (even though our freedom is given us by God).

On the first page of God's holy book we read: "And subdue it [the earth]." Christians could not foresee—and had no need to do so—what a history and what challenges lay hidden in those words. But when we know that we are endowed with our freedom and our direct relationship to God, when we have understood that all things visible are not God but are mere creatures and inferior to man, God's partner, so that man stands beside God over against crea-

tion and in the God-Man has even become God's am-
bassador to nature, then clearly this man, this Christian,
was bound to discover one day that the fundamental
Christian relation to the world and nature exists not
merely in the inwardness of faith, conscience and prayer
but also in and through the world itself, in the fact of
knowledge by earthly science and the ensuing subjection
of nature.

And so the Christian may regard this primal and necessary evolution as a challenge he must face, as the defense
and vindication of his dignity as the creature of God and
the amnestied partner of God.

A New Testament recollection may well be appended
here. When the scribes said to Jesus that he, a mere man,
was making himself God, he replied: "Is it not written
in your law, 'I said, you are gods'?" (Jn. 10, 33f.). The
Roman liturgy says: "O God, who hast wonderfully created man in his dignity and yet more wonderfully renewed
him, grant us by this mingling [of water and wine] to
share in the divinity of him who was pleased to share in
our humanity."

Now what implications does the character of the present human situation have for religion? With this question
we arrive at the crux of our whole subject.

Let us begin by admitting that at first sight, and
probably at first experience too, this situation makes
religious dealings with God considerably more difficult.
God seems to have drawn farther away from man since
man's exploits have, as it were, turned nature into the
material of his own creative activity. While the world
has fallen under man's control thanks to the discovery
and manipulation of its laws, it seems for just that reason
to be a solid wall separating man from God. In nature and

what he makes out of it, man seems to find only the world
—the laws of matter and his own reflection.

Of course it can always be said that this very world is
God's creation, that the laws man discovers are laws laid
down by God, and that what man himself does he does in
virtue of a free spiritual nature which the same God has
created and called by name. All well and good—but it
does not change the fact that this world is now more remote from God insofar as contemporary man is concerned.
What happens in it is no longer experienced so much—at
least no longer so directly and intensely—as the activity
of God in and for the world. Miracles are no longer met
with every day; an extraordinary phenomenon means
little more than a challenge to science to explain it and
thus degrade it into something ordinary. The wretchedness
of this world no longer moves men to entreat nature's
Lord in prayer but only to fight its forces still more
desperately until they are vanquished or checked. The
world remains godless, profane, hominized, conformed to
man—although again the inhumanity of man himself may
stare at us, out of this hominized world, in the shape of
ravaged nature, atomic, bacteriological and chemical
weapons, and other horrors, the worst of which is the
depersonalization of men for the benefit of a few rulers.
And in the first place this godless, hominized world does
mean that God is remote, that the idea of him has grown
dim and unreal, alien to earth, that God has dropped out
of our categories.

Trying to say that besides nature and far above it we
have God's own revealed Word in Scripture is no help.
Scripture calls God the creator of the world (Gen. 1) who
can be known as such (Rom. 1, 20); heaven is "God's
throne" and earth "his footstool" (Mt. 5, 35); God is the

benefactor who "gives rains from heaven and fruitful
seasons" (Acts 14, 17), "of whose glory the earth is full"
(Ps. 56, 12) —although he "hangs the earth upon nothing"
(Job 26, 7). But before we can so much as begin to hear
or read this Word of God, we have long been caught up
in this world of today; we are already skeptics, rationalists,
men with an instinct for scientific and historical origins
and explanations. We feel that Scripture itself is primarily
an echo of a bygone world, an utterance made in the
language peculiar to a world picture which has now grown
strange to us; and it is only by dint of much labor, with an
aching mind and heart, that we manage to translate Scripture into our own language so that it may not seem a
mere monument of an age in the history of religions that
has long been dead.

But if this rationalist and technological secularism of
the West more and more dominates the one world of all
nations and individuals, and if this inescapable fact springs
from a *Christian* origin, as we have said, then this pro-
fanity of the world (which seems to leave the world godless and God worldless) simply must have some positive
significance and present us with a religious task which it
behooves us to take in hand. Such indeed is the case.

In the first place, even today man's world remains
ultimately uncontrollable, a world whose future is
shrouded in mists. It is not only that our world imposes
its laws on man even today, not only that the material with
which man creates remains rough and brittle even today,
so that his creativity is revealed to be creaturely and is
endured as such, and not only that man in all his power
is a poor dying thing and in the most up-to-date clinics
experiences the utter denial of his absolute autonomy.

There is something quite different besides. Not unconquered, unbounded nature alone but man's own creation, too, impresses it upon him that he himself is subject to control. Do not man's proudest, best-laid plans hurry him, even today, into an unforeseeable, astonishing, unplanned future? Does not man find himself, today more than ever, exposed to an existential anguish which proves that his planned, controlled activity still—indeed more than ever—somehow turns into enduring an unintelligible fate? Is man's freedom not always the venturing into a future of impenetrable darkness? Have not even the communist planners of a rational future settled for planning the next few years at best—planning without foreknowing them? And does this not happen of necessity because every act of freedom presents itself once again before the dark freedom of this world's mighty ones (at least in a succeeding generation), who in their turn regard that planning and execution as material for a new decision which always selects *one* out of many possibilities.

In truth man still dwells in the land of the uncontrollable. Uncontrollable nature has been turned into a world of man, his own work, indeed, and on that very account all the darker, all the more sinister. Man experiences himself as one who is ever opening up the uncontrollable in freedom. He may still be intoxicated with the freedom from nature which he has won, but it will soon become more and more clear to him (it is already clear to wise men today) that his creative freedom experiences itself as subject to control and as venturing into unfathomable darkness.

Now to *whom* shall man entrust this subject state of all things? Whence shall he receive it? Where shall he know his freedom to be hidden as it ventures forward, plunging into darkness? If mystery no longer confronts

him so plainly and directly in the nature which surrounds
him, it is now welling up out of his own nature. We call
this mystery God. And the more we become what we are,
free beings endowed with a certain degree of power, the
more we seek him to whom this subject lordship, which
never belongs to ourselves, can be entrusted—God.

Moreover, the more powerful man becomes, the more
he subjects nature to himself, the heavier grows his
responsibility, the more utterly he is exposed to himself,
the farther his capacities reach beyond his immediate
circle to affect the destiny of more and more human beings,
and the more responsible each becomes for all. It is a
truism that mankind's moral progress has failed to keep
pace with its scientific, technical and cultural progress,
so that one of the possibilities which the future holds is
a flood of barbarism and ruin—how far away or how near,
none can tell.

A man who has his wits about him can learn brand-
new lessons from this situation whereby the things we
create escape our control; he can learn how heavy responsibility is and what a serious matter life is. It is not that
man in the age of science and technology is necessarily a
less civilized and less moral specimen. The attitude of
objectivity, modesty, responsibility and quiet usefulness
is one that is expected and taken "professionally" in the
world of modern science and technology, and where such
responsibility is felt to be unconditional and is practiced
as such, we have a genuine relationship with God, though
it may not bear that name. For the ultimate, absolute
principle of all responsibility is called God. That silent
listening for what we ought to do is a listening to God.
And by God I mean precisely him whom we encounter
(though perhaps we give him no name and out of timidity

avoid looking at him) by recognizing our actual freedom as an enormous burden that bears down upon us and that we do not cravenly dodge.

A third thing needs to be said—namely that human creativity today is capable of nurturing religion, the germ of faith conceived in the inward man, and keeping it in view as man goes about his business.

We have seen how men of earlier ages were more at nature's mercy than we are, but for that very reason nature to them was a mother from whom they could expect more gentleness than rigor, and some pleasant surprises. Chance could be dealt with by magic, and luck, fortune with her horn of plenty, could be relied on. Today, of course, there are still "chance" happenings, lucky and unlucky, but generally speaking the world of contemporary man has become a sober, practical one. Man suffers from the worldliness of his world, from its unpredictability (despite the mathematical symbols of the initiate) ; he suffers from the world he himself has made. On closer scrutiny we find that it is because of the finitude, hazards and mortality of human life. In short, the harsh reality of this human world, the new cruelty that man cannot help communicating to his own world if it is to be viable, would seem to be only a new form of man's mortality, his exposure to death. "Man that is born of a woman is of few days and full of trouble. He comes forth like a flower, and withers; he flees like a shadow and continues not. And thou hast appointed his bounds that he cannot pass" (Job 14, 1. 2. 5). "And God said to man, 'Behold, the fear of the Lord, that is wisdom; and to depart from evil is understanding'" (Job 28, 28).

If this be the case, then one can say in truth that voluntary endurance of this harsh reality, over which we have little or no control, is a *participation in the sufferings and death of Christ*. Today we are not only destined to die when life ends (a fact that is as hard now as it ever was); this dying in the midst of life is the permanent residue with which man today is left for his pains, even as regards the conquest of nature. A wise man today knows that he is always dying; he meets death in the cold harshness of the world which we have made for ourselves and which now emerges as the pain we must inflict on ourselves in order to survive. Now if he accepts this situation, then wittingly or not he shares in the saving death throes of the redeemer. For the death of the Lord is precisely the hopeless situation which turns to victory because it has been accepted by God himself.

There is more. As we have already mentioned, the present age, however much it has been distorted by sin and infidelity, is not only not un-Christian in its underlying structure but actually rests upon Christian foundations. Christianity has delivered the world from the numinous and from magic, making it the material with which man works, and thus for the first time man has become what he is meant to be, a free subject before God, answerable for himself even in the domain of earthly things and nature. It is only on this basis that God achieves his full stature in men's eyes as the creator, infinitely exalted above all things, dwelling in his own glory which is inaccessible to us. And so it follows that a positive, creative relation to the world can perfectly well be experienced and accepted as an element of Christianity.

No doubt Christianity remains level-headed and critical about this sense of life. It knows that anything can become a curse to man if he arrogantly locks God out of his heart. But a Christian has no reason to be any more critical and wary about the new sense of life than about the "good old days." The old and the new "world is in the power of the evil one," as John says (1 Jn. 5, 19) —the new one no more so than the old, although the wider scope it offers for human action means that abuse can become monstrous.

God has made the world an evolving world, a world of change and growth; only in man and his creative deeds does it become what God means it to be: the world of man which, changeable, fleeting and sinful though it is, has been granted a share in the life of God by the God-Man. Thus it is not readily apparent why a Christian should consider the human situation in this new age more dangerous, less capable of leading men to God, than that of earlier ages. The world is always God's world, even though full of temptation and human guilt. It can draw men away from God but also draw them to him. Of course a Christian, too, can get bogged down in this world, but he will not find God by trying to take refuge in an age that is dead or dying.

Two more points deserve consideration. First, we must state more bluntly than we have done so far that this profane world, though not an "anointed" one, is nevertheless a *sanctified* world. What we call grace, the interior divinization of God's image and likeness which wells out from the core of his being and openness to God's immediacy, does not wait for explicit preaching of the faith, for the Church's sacraments and worship and the written Word of God. From the beginning God has accepted and sanctified the *whole* world and all its dimensions—but in such a way that God's grace, in order to leave scope for man's freedom, is always at variance with guilt, mankind as it concretely exists always remaining a compound of

God's "yes" and man's "no." Nor does the Church exactly coincide with sanctified mankind. In the world of today it may be hard to discover the mystery of God's absolute closeness, but it is everywhere and will abide until the end of the world.

The Church herself, in her relation to this world, is still very much in the making. This is so in the abstract because the dialogue of theology with the view of life which the men of this world take needs working up and renewing, and it is so in the concrete because the Church can still give up a good many time-honored positions which have had their day. After all, the institutional Church cannot deal directly with every ethical question that arises and every ethical answer that is sought in the sphere of man's creative powers today. This does not mean that the Church is surrendering to an arbitrary view of life held by men today, retreating from a purely profane world into a purely sacred sphere. But it does mean that the Christian layman is being taken seriously as a witness of the Church in the world. The profane is not identical with the sacred, yet each finds its perfection only in the other. No man can unite the two domains, but every Christian is constantly summoned, graciously called to be at once secular and suprasecular, at once to act in the world and to act by the leading of the Spirit.

The conclusion has already been hinted at: the experience of man's creative power is inseparable from the experience that this man-made world slips away into a new uncontrollability, into a responsibility of horrifying proportions. Man experiences himself as the one who must "go forth" to many things—without ever being able to achieve control of all things—in order to bring himself into play. Man experiences himself as a mere rough draft which is swallowed up in a mystery—and by that very fact man also experiences what is really meant by God: that mystery of infinite, unutterable, blinding plenitude which appoints the beginning, ensures the stubborn oneness of the whole and takes up the perfecting of a man's life which eludes the man himself, if only he has worked hard at it with this mystery in view.

"Then Job answered the Lord: 'I know that thou canst do all things. . . . I will question you, and you declare to me. I had heard of thee . . . but now my eye sees thee'" (Job 42, 1f., 5).

V

Science and Faith

How are knowledge and faith related? One may start by considering knowledge—that is, the world picture of contemporary natural science. The procedure is legitimate if only because we cannot do otherwise in this world and therefore in its view of the world. But lest the impression be given that this is the stable, obvious, self-sufficient connection, we must also ask conversely how the connection looks when it is considered from the point of view of faith.

Man finds himself already in the world when he begins to reflect seriously about his life, begins to take it upon himself. This world is not simply a world of facts, if for no other reason than that facts exist for us only as known —that is, in perceptions and opinions. The world in which we found ourselves at the start is a world of knowledge, opinions, ideas and convictions, and of standards and conduct based thereon. In short, it has already been established as a world picture by earlier generations. We begin with an inherited world picture, and this ready-made world picture in our minds, which we can never quite shake off, has two aspects: one metaphysical and one historical.

The world picture pre-exists in a metaphysical sense.

This means that every attempt which can be made to construct a world picture out of our actual experience with things rests from the outset on all kinds of metaphysical, pre-empirical assumptions which seem to us universally valid and which nevertheless do not really admit of empirical proof. For instance one can inquire: Is there such a thing as reality, and if so in what sense? Has every cause a definite effect, and, conversely, is there an adequate reason for everything? Such antecedent structures of thought and being prove to be sound and convincing in any given case only for a man who freely relies on them. There is no ground outside these assumptions from which a man can judge and direct the whole course of thought.

But there are also historical presuppositions to all our thought which can never be completely eliminated. Each and every one of us (it is the same yesterday, today, or tomorrow) begins with a ready-made, inherited world picture. And this is true not only of philosophical principles, even if we undertake to examine and improve the world picture, as natural scientists of course do. Even if we look with the utmost suspicion on our world picture and the philosophical principles it implies, we are not free of it. Even while protesting against it we are still probing into and protesting against an antecedent reality that confronts us. We could only build up a complete and independent view of things for ourselves if we contrived never to have listened to another man, never to have spoken an inherited language, never to have read a book, and yet to get beyond the experience of a newborn babe. No, despite being a person and despite his freedom, man can no more do away with the assumptions of his intellectual existence than he can do away with his biological inheritance.

Thus man's world picture is historical by nature. This

is *also* true of the natural scientist's world picture, for
that picture, too, is antecedently shaped and affects not
this or that feature alone but even the selection of the
themes that science will consider, and above all the direction of scientific inquiry. The standard of selection in
natural science is historically conditioned and moreover,
as a principle, cannot be an object of pure natural science.
A scientist discovers only what can be discovered along the
route which his voyage of discovery has taken. But the
direction of the scientist's inquiring gaze is not determined
by the object (because that has not yet been apprehended)
but by an antecedent decision, whether that of the investi-
gator's "scientific curiosity" or that of a commercial enter-
prise or a government which is sponsoring the experiment.
Not even the eventual success of the discovery proves that
it was the right thing on which to embark. The discovery
can never tell us what was forgotten or passed by and
whether that would not have been of more importance.
(One has only to think of certain atomic tests and their
dubious character when ethics as well as science is taken
into account.) But neither an individual nor an historical
era can break new ground in all directions at once, so as
to discover everything and give everything due consideration. Thus every "conquest" involves a renunciation or
loss as well, and a blessing may turn out to be a curse.
The only question is what natural science can renounce
by its conquests without the renunciation proving fatal.

Therefore, man has a world picture based on metaphysical and historical assumptions. A variety of elements
enters into the making of his world picture, elements
which are drawn from knowledge and social intercourse
and which combine to set the stage for existence. A "world
picture" is the mirror reflecting a limited being who is
conditioned by many factors.

Now the truth of religion, belief in God and God's historical revelation in Jesus Christ, is also antecedent to the scientific world picture. Faith springs from a more primal source in human existence than does scientific reflection. The truth of religion (as we shall demonstrate at greater length) occupies the same place in human existence as the presuppositions of science. Therefore it is not for the scientific world picture to sit in judgment on religion.

Of course there are no double truths—truths, that is, which contradict each other—and if conflict arises, then both sides must honestly ask themselves just where the source of conflict lies. But in this matter religion is not simply at the mercy of science and the scientific world picture. Religion derives from a source which is loftier because it is earlier and springs from a more primal kind of living. Let us now enlarge upon this matter.

Man makes his own world picture for himself; he knows that in this world picture of his he is finite and that he faces an endless range of inquiries and potentialities there in the background of finitude. Thus he is not only related to his world picture as to the appointed sphere, already hedged in by himself, of what can be directly investigated; he is also related first and last to what does *not* belong to that sphere, to what stands in the background of the world picture and yet discloses the abiding finitude and historicity of his world and its image, ungrasped and ungraspable. The unutterable is the source of all his utterance. That for which there is no picture makes his world picture possible. The objective primal source of everything real is present without forming part of our world picture. And this objective primal source is the goal, unattainable by us in its own nature, (the "to which") of all we do to construct a world picture. We call it God.

Accordingly, knowledge of God is antecedently different in nature from the knowledge with which we put together a world picture. God is not part of the world, but its presupposition. He is not one objective bit of knowledge among others; he is the infinity which is always there beforehand in the motions of our knowing, and the motions of our knowing run their ever finite course within this infinity. God is not the concluding thesis deduced from the preliminary draft of a complete world picture, but rather the one thesis in all the hypotheses of our world picture. Moreover, when men construct a world picture, always and everywhere the particular structure rests on the assumption that the plurality of earthly things exhibits a meaning, a cohesion, a correlation, so that a primal, meaningful oneness precedes the plurality. The limitations and dubiety of a world picture from which all science draws sustenance can themselves only be known through an antecedent and implicit affirmation of an infinite being, aimed at indeed but thinkable only by analogy (an image that is like and unlike). We call that being God.

Thus all picturing of the world, all intellectual grasping and ordering of the plurality of things, is done by reaching forth to the unimaginable, the incomprehensible, to what is not part of the world or of any world picture but stands, infinite, behind all the plurality of earthly things. We call that God.

As that to which knowledge of the world is ordered and that from which the world comes forth, this infinitude is not objectively thinkable; it can only be a spiritual, subsistent, personal being.

Such has always been the burden of Christian philosophy. It has always said that God is not part of the world, of that which can be experienced and understood; he is not even the keystone of them, but rather what the world and knowledge of the world presuppose. Man cannot directly gaze at this presupposition with his mind's eye; he cannot directly make it an object of his intellect. Rather, he always knows it indirectly, as the infinite, in that experience of the multifarious and the conditional refers him to the absolute without bringing that absolute into the ambit of human thought or direct experience.

As we have observed, Christian philosophers have always known this truth. But (odd as the question may sound) have they always *spoken* accordingly? In principle they knew the truth, but to make it count in their sense of reality, their experience and their practical living, used to be difficult. For theirs was a small world—or rather, their world picture was so modest and simple that its tale was soon told, so simple with respect to space and time that one very soon felt that he knew everything, and God, in one's experience, became practically part of the world. God was in heaven, yes; but he was there as in a spatial extension of the world. Today all this has changed through an alteration, an incalculable deepening of the world picture. The world presents itself as something complete in itself which refers men to God only as a whole (abstracting, first of all, from the supernatural event of redemption). And because this world as a whole speaks primarily and directly of itself, only bearing dumb witness to God, many people suppose that God cannot be found. For one seems to find only more and more of the world, the more one probes into it. In reality, however, this experience does not prove the soundness of atheism; it proves the fact that the world is not God.

Toward the end of the 18th century and during the

19th there existed a theoretical and practical atheism which claimed (so naïve and shallow it was) to know that there is no God. Though it has only become a mass phenomenon in our own day, and the dogma of a militant political philosophy, this atheism remains essentially a thing of the past. This is not true of what we shall call "unconcerned atheism." Terror at God's absence from the world, the feeling that one can no longer really experience the divine, dismay at God's silence, his withdrawnness into his own inaccessibility, the senseless drive to make the world entirely profane, the matter-of-factness of the world's laws where not nature but man is concerned —any experience of this type makes people think that they must profess themselves to be atheists.

However, such is a genuine experience (even though it be partly involved with a wrong interpretation), an experience which the Christian mind has by no means thought through. Fundamentally it is only a realization that God does not belong in the world picture, that he is not the mainspring in the clockwork of the world, that events which are part of the world's "normal" course can always be found to spring from a cause that is not God. Now this experience is not atheism but conveys a truth which coincides with the principle of St. Thomas Aquinas: In the natural order God does everything through causes that are not himself.[1] What we are really dealing with here is a maturing of the image of God in the human mind. We now experience through and through what we always knew in the abstract, what Vatican Council I teaches and we passed off rather glibly: that God is infinitely exalted above all that is outside him and can be conceived of him. If this is so—and it is part of the marrow

[1] Teilhard de Chardin expresses the same thought in *Die Schau in die Vergangenheit* (Olten, 1965), pp. 40-41, and in other works.

of Christian faith—then God is exalted above all earthly
utterance; he does not fit into it; one can speak of him
only in a language that is qualitatively different.

Mankind today is experiencing this truth, for it is
gradually assimilating a scientific world picture as profane
as the world, which is not God himself and above which
he is infinitely exalted, so that no similarity exists between
it and him which does not prove to be that much more of
a dissimilarity[2]. God's truth and our image of the world
are two different things. Only today are we learning that
no image of God can be carved in the wood of the world.
It behooves the educated man of today to accept this
experience, which is at once pain and grace. To suppress
that duty, for the sake of a human image of God, in an
overhasty apologetics, would be absurd. This experience
must be rightly interpreted—that is, we must understand
that it has nothing to do with atheism.

With a tranquil mind let us admit the anguish of
faith. There is no harm in doing so. We do not, like
children, experience God as ruling the world. Men of
earlier ages were able to do so; we are not. It is not as
though God were dead, but he is greater, nameless, incomprehensible. "God *is*": this is not a proposition which
could be added to the other propositions laid down by
science. "God *is*": this proposition is more primal than
any affirmation of the world, because (whether heard or
unheard) it is already enunciated when, dazed, we begin
to ask in the sciences how we can think through the world
we find ourselves in, and name it so as to master it. The
proposition "God *is*" is of an entirely different nature
from propositions such as "our earth is" or "technology
is." It is audible in all other propositions, but for that
very reason it may always be drowned out by all other

2 Denzinger, *Enchiridion Symbolorum*, 432.

propositions. For in our scientific, empirical knowledge of the world the subject "God" figures only as the subject of other propositions, never as such and on its own *among* the other subjects. That is why God is so far away and we are so far away from him—because he is the unconditioned and illimitable, whereas we are conditioned and our knowledge is designed to understand things by limiting them. The world picture, with the creaturely, finite truth proper to it, is the sum of the utterable, the delimitable and the calculable, whereas absolute truth, which is God, conveys that he is the incomprehensible and that his magnitude will not fit into the fields and systems of coordinates that we devise, into this net of finitude in which we catch the world.

Such knowledge cannot have the rational exactitude of that knowledge with which we build up today's world picture—not because the former is less reliable and hazier than the latter but because it is a knowledge that has the undelimitable for its object, a knowledge which possesses itself of us instead of our possessing ourselves of it, a knowledge whereby we do not grasp but are grasped, whereby the only obvious thing is said, and which therefore is incomprehensible to us.

If great intellectual processes hold their meaning and their promise despite the obstinate guilt and folly of men, then so does the anguish of faith, our age's existential dread. It is the dread that God might be lost to us, a strangling emotion which does not arise solely from the malice and shallowness, the pride and moral guilt of men. This dread, too, has its meaning: God is becoming greater. He is withdrawing to a distance which makes it possible for the first time to see that our mind's eye cannot take him in. We can feel a brotherly closeness, not indeed to militant atheists but to people who are distressed by the

problem of God, quiet, self-contained people who do not
care for noisy zeal. We have all besought the mute incomprehensibility of God, whether under that name or
not. In them and us alike the most accurate world picture
as a whole is a problem that does not solve itself. They and
we alike have known something of the distress in that
cry: "My God, my God, why hast thou forsaken me?" As
to them, we think (having no right to judge them as
persons) : they only *think;* they do not believe. As to
ourselves, we know that we correctly express what they
know in the depths of their mind and conscience, too,
without their being able to put it into so many words:
that everything is embraced, sustained and beheld by the
necessarily unutterable mystery which we call God.

This is the truth of truths, the truth that "makes men
free" and opens them. Without it all finitude, all the
accurate detail there is in the world picture, becomes the
dungeon in which man dies the death of an animal (a
clever animal).

This one truth, that God *is*, opens the door to the
incomprehensible, to a domain where we do not control
but are controlled, do not master but adore. We are
brought into a region where of ourselves we cannot find
the roads, where we are controlled by a fate we do not
steer. But the courage—or, let us rather say, the serene
and confident love—with which a man entrusts himself to
this incomprehensibility is a deed, *the* deed whereby he
affirms his inmost being.

Now of course by distinguishing the world picture and
God's truth in this way and yet associating them, we have
not said the last word about what we profess as Christians.
Christianity, after all, is not simply mute adoration of
the nameless God. It rests upon *knowledge* of God, com-
municated by the God-Man Jesus Christ, by his redemp-

tive work and message; it lives in an institutional Church which is endowed with Word and sacrament, with the great commandment of love, with many ordinances and many forms of devotion. Of course apparent contradictions and conflicts can arise between the modern scientific world picture and religious belief. And they may arise more often than if we were dealing simply with an intellectual belief in God on the one hand and the contemporary world picture on the other. For certain though it be that God's Word is *God's* Word and exists antecedent to scientific elaboration of our earthly experience, nevertheless the truth of God's Word is expressed in human concepts and human language. Now these are partly shaped by the world picture and work with images drawn from the realm of human experience. Thus, for instance, the Bible uses such images as "sons" of God, divine "generation" and God's "wrath"; the history of dogma speaks of a change in the "substance" of bread, of a divine "nature" in three "persons," of "infused" virtues—so many illustrations of the fact that God's Word has entered human language and savors of this earth—and inevitably so if men are to understand it. The Lord himself "spoke to the crowds in parables; indeed he said nothing to them without a parable." We obviously cannot work out a theology of verbal revelation here, and it is hardly necessary to enlarge upon the connection between Christian teaching and natural science. In these matters the apparent conflict between the two authorities has really been disposed of. But some may find a few additional remarks helpful.

First let us say a word about religious terminology. I suppose that we, the heirs of 19th-century rationalism, are especially aware today, in this age of technology and the exact sciences, that our human concepts as applied to God and his truth are images, analogies (that is, both compare and contrast with him). This is made clear to us as it was not to earlier, more primitive men. We hardly use such expressions now as God "roars" (Jer. 25, 30) or "God was sorry that he had made man" (Gen. 6, 6) — images that the Old Testament prophets uttered almost instinctively. Whether or not we should congratulate ourselves on shrinking from the use of them, in many ways it is our destiny to shrink from such "imagist" human language about God, and it can also prove a blessing. For to understand that God is the incomprehensible being, exalted above all we can say of him, is a grace and a blessing—won by dint of sorrow. We make our way "through shadows and images to the truth" (as the epitaph says which Cardinal Newman composed for himself). But that is no reason for doubting the meaningfulness and weight of what our affirmations indicate, the knowledge of which matters more than all earthly knowledge. To stammer about God, to be able to stammer about him and in his presence, is more important than discoursing accurately about the world. And frankly, much of the offense which modern educated laymen take at such formularies springs from their lack of a solid theological background. Christian theology is well aware that its concepts are analogical and takes pains to make the meaning of the formularies perceptible. One must agree, of course, that not every priest is able to clarify their content, but then neither is every machinist able to say something pertinent about nuclear physics. An educated Christian will not suppose that if he finds some difficulty about the meaning of a dogma, theologians can never have given it any thought. And obviously to think that one must dispel the mystery would be naïve; it would be a sign that one has fallen into a rationalist misinterpretation of divine truth.

Within the framework of this likeness and unlikeness

that mark human notions of God there is one area, biblical language, which is felt to be particularly unsuitable today because it presupposes the old world picture. Hence the demand, especially among Protestant theologians, for "demythologization." When we say that God is "in heaven," that the Son of God "came down to earth," "descended into hell" (to the underworld of the departed) and "ascended into heaven," when we read the imagery in the Apocalypse about the end of the world, about stars on fire and falling from heaven, all this certainly presupposes a world picture that is not ours pure and simple. The same applies to the naïve idea of God's immanence in the world which has already been discussed. But it does not follow that such statements need to be "demythologized." The reasons are two. In the first place these statements by no means become meaningless even if the world picture reflected in their language falls away. And in the second place even the sense which was intended in those days remains unaffected. The inspiration of the Spirit does not vouch for the world picture in which the statement is set as within a frame. True, the human authors made no allowance for the possibility of a different world picture; they were unaware of the possibility. When we are told, for instance, that he "was taken up into heaven," this statement is certainly made in full accordance with the old world picture; it affirms a spatial movement from earth to the dwelling-"place" of the blessed. And yet what it means is the new "state."

Nor are there any dogmas that stand or fall with the old world picture. Very little reflection is necessary in order to perceive the changeless meaning of the "descent into hell" or of "sitting at the right hand of God the Father." There is surely no difficulty about understanding that Scripture means the redemptive power of the God-

Man alike for those generations which have gone before
and for those which are to come, and the beatitude of his
own human nature in God. And set within our present
world picture those statements surely become less vivid,
if not less meaningful, than they were for the ancients,
whose imagination connected the heavenly state with a
place on high, above the stars.

Two points must not be overlooked, however. First,
the growing obscurity of such religious statements is par-
alleled by the scientific consciousness, whose knowledge
can indeed be expressed in mathematical formulae but
becomes more and more obscure. Second, the experiential
impact of the obscure is not bound to dwindle in the long
run. God used to be the most obscure thing on earth, and
he still is; nevertheless, believers experience him all the
more clearly as the highest good, no less today than in
former times. As time goes on there is less danger of
naïvely gelding religious truths and turning God into a
mere human being.

Finally, one more consideration as to the present state
of affairs follows from the primacy of religion as an experiential relationship with God, from the inclusion of
divine revelation in the scentific world picture and from
the mysterious nature of human existence even for
scientists.

The leading spirits of the 19th century thought that
human existence could be governed by pure reason;
reason set the tone in everything that matters to man.
Thus a famous chemist was able to call chemistry his
"religious affiliation." Today that scientific faith is dying.
It has been shown that making science the explanation of
life is overstraining it, that the scientific world picture
depends on a picture of man, and that both before and
after natural science come metaphysics and faith, both of

them essentially ordered to decision, to freedom. If it be
true that behind the Iron Curtain the philosophizing is
done for reasons of State, it is also true that the West will
not overcome the unbelief of the East (which is a faith and
not science) with 19th-century science and nothing else.
It should always have been clear that man cannot live by
science alone. Science is reflection; antecedent to reflection
there exists something metaphysical and historical which
beyond all doubt guides the course of science, always and
of necessity. This something can never be quite caught
up with. And therefore the reflection of science cannot
possibly be the root of human existence.

The consequence is of the utmost importance: if
science (which is good and willed by God) is not to
become a poisonous, aimless business of know-alls, a
curiosity that distracts us from the heart of existence,
then the *root* of our primal, unarticulated understanding
of and with life must not be cut off, but must grow deeper
into its source and ground in proportion as science
branches out into the vastness of the empirical.

Failing this serene, confident understanding with the
source and ground of existence, with God in prayer and
practical willingness to serve, a man may know many
things but his house is built on sand. With a thousand
truths but without "the one thing necessary," life becomes
absurd to the depths. There are moments of doubt and
distress, and for those moments the Lord gave us the
admonition: "Pray that you may not enter into temptation" (Mk. 14, 38).

Praying helps us have the courage to believe, and
belief is demanded of each one of us.

VI

Is Faith an Ideology?

THE crucial question in the title of this chapter is put to Christian philosophy, with its first and peremptory proposition "God is," as contrasted with a philosophy, and its corresponding existential tone and attitude to life, where man shuts himself against that first truth. First of all, let us observe that more is involved in the Christian credo than mere knowledge, mere assent to the truth of a thesis. In Christian worship "I believe" ("credo") is said as a prayer of the community, as praise of God who has revealed himself in Jesus Christ, just as friendship, love and acceptance of one's ties with society and the State involve more than an intellectual knowledge. Mere knowledge does not automatically imply its existential embodiment: "Even the demons believe—and shudder" (Jas. 2, 19). The "credo" deals with fundamentals in the relationship of the whole man to that supreme mystery which we call God, and the very knowledge it contains, says the Council of Orange (A.D. 528), comes from an illumination of grace (Denz. 180-182).

The objections put forward against Christian faith, founded on faith in God, ultimately spring from a skeptical or relativist outlook. When the scope of reality is

arbitrarily confined to what natural science and technology can prove, all other reality is dismissed as a figment
of the imagination, as the "opiate of the people" or the
like. Therefore Christianity or any other religion is a
utopian idealization of human life—wishful thinking, the
fruit of our imperious longing for a complete and noble
explanation of existence. But obviously this whole idea
presupposes an ideology which can only accept one kind
of being.

It has often been possible to misinterpret Christianity
as an ideology because it allowed itself to become the
vassal of particular cultures, of particular economic or
political interests, and was then combatted by the oppos-
ing cultures and interests. For human nature is such that
it can draw even faith into the half-light of an ideology.

A still graver danger of misunderstanding arises from
the necessity of communicating the real content of Christianity, the mystery of God and his redemption, through
historical symbols and ecclesiastical arrangements, so that
it is easy to misconstrue the communication of invisible,
spiritual things in visible garb as a mere device of the
human mind with religious decorations, instead of God's
ordinance.

Another reason why people tend to look on Christianity as an ideology is the existence of so many religions in
the form of faith or of philosophy. This phenomenon
enables us to understand the skeptical relativism whereby
people hold all religions to be equally valuable or equally
worthless. When natural science inclines contemporary
man to take for granted the universal validity of a genuine
truth and his democratic instincts encourage him to credit
everyone with approximately as much intelligence and
good will as he himself has, almost inevitably he will be
astonished and upset by the existence of many different

philosophies, and then he may well jump to the conclusion that anything lying beyond exact knowledge of the mathematical and scientific sort is optional, at best of subjective significance. And he will judge the Christian religion accordingly.

But obviously such a transposition from one plane to another is objectively unsound. Just as the good mathematician or natural scientist is not automatically a good man as well—and if he happens to be, then that is not because he is a brilliant mathematician or a learned and ingenious scientist—so it is in the domain of the sacred. Faith as the foundation of religious reverence toward that which is above all things can certainly not be identified with mathematical thought or scientific experimentation, nor even with sheer ethics, although a brilliant mathematician or ingenious scientist may at the same time be a man of high moral caliber and even a man sanctified by grace.

Now to get down to our real subject. It should not take more than a few moments to distinguish belief in God, especially Christian belief, from ideology. In the first place faith in God is not ideology because it is concerned with an affirmation, in the simplest sense of the word, about invisible mystery. This affirmation can be called metaphysical to the extent that, though absolutely true, it does not rest upon empirical, scientific proofs. If one cares to say that belief in God is true because it is important to human life, fair enough. But to dismiss everything that transcends the senses and pure reason as a dream and then to ask why faith nevertheless has its importance for human life is to apply a metaphysics (all unawares) to something which is not purely rational—and a bad metaphysics at that if the object of all faith is pronounced unreal, so that only "irrational" people re-

main capable of such fancies. Were faith an ideology, it
would logically follow that believers are dolts lost in a
dream. Still, metaphysics, which is thinking with ideas,
need not therefore be considered suspect as an ideology.
To say that it must is itself to put forward a metaphysical
thesis. Relativism and skepticism are metaphysical decisions. Reflection about experiences within the realm of
our existence is inevitably done in ideas on which man is
dependent, as a thinking being, for the interpretation of
his particular subjective experiences. And ultimately these
ideas refer him to a source in which they converge: that
mystery ever present since before time was, namely God.
This bedrock of human existence, bestowed in knowledge
and responsible freedom, is not apprehended in itself by
sensory perception or by ideas but rather lays hold on the
inward man. We call it grace (favor) as God's loving
self-communication and self-attestation in the creative
Spirit (Rom. 8, 16) or in the "heart" as the sum of man's
thinking, feeling and willing (Ez. 18, 31; Rom. 10, 10;
Gal. 4, 6 and *passim*). It is the interior encounter with
God when he "draws" a man (Hos. 11, 4; Jn. 6, 44),
called faith; it is a going forth from oneself in acknowledgment of one's own guilt, in a surrender of the self because
one trusts in God's forgiveness and is prepared to do his
will insofar as he knows it. This grace of faith connotes a
participation in the life of God, of him who is exalted
above all things. Faith is offered to all men because of
God's universal salvific will, a will that always remains the
same, even where man deliberately shuts himself against
God (Wis. 11, 23–12, 2; 1 Tim. 2, 4).

All this, taken together, means that in the depth of
his personal being man is sustained by God himself and
impelled to direct contact with God. In other words, what
we call grace is the openness of the personal spirit to God,

granted by God himself—the authentically human attitude, the interior capacity for and fact of receiving God, through his self-communication, at the core of our existence. It is the most authentic of supermundane experience, the religious experience of God's absolute, forgiving intimacy, the inmost union with God in the "spark of the soul" (to use the figure of the ancients), with the holy, adorable mystery that is different from and exalted above all things: God. Thus ideology is left far behind. For every ideology is concerned with matters of earthly experience, verifiable as such, whether this earthly experience be called "blood and soil," technological mastery of the forces of nature, the fashionable world of one's own inanity and nothingness, or whatever the basic mundane features of purely human existence are. Asserting its absolute claim to man, Christianity interprets all this as "idols of this world," as "principalities and powers" of unredeemed existence. What matters in faith is always that man at the core of his being shall be open to the "other world," to the proffered direct contact with God, beyond all natural experience, to the grace-given motion of eternal life in God and nearer to God which must be affirmed by man's free acts.

At the same time Christianity is essentially history. Its belief in God is rooted in God's saving deeds whereby he bears witness to himself in the people of Israel—a series of deeds reaching from Abraham, through Moses and the prophets, to Jesus Christ. Thus history is part of the very nature of Christianity, that divinely ordained, unmistakable series of God's attestations to himself and to grace through the calling of his witnesses, the conquest of this world's false gods in divine chastisement and the forgiveness of sin. And on the horizontal plane of historical governance both reach fulfillment in Christianity as the

New Covenant. What stamps Christianity is a saving deed wrought in history by the God-Man for all who will be disciples until the end of time—something absolutely unique, in no way comparable with ideologies offered for men to choose among. Christian faith is built upon God's historical redemption in the God-Man Jesus Christ and its presence down the ages in signs of grace. Therefore, it can never be superseded by any human ideology or by any of the philosophic systems that come and go, though a certain importance may attach to these; it can never be superseded by any other religion, even though, thanks to God's guidance of redemptive history, other religions may also partake of Christ in one respect or another.

Thus faith in God in the name of Jesus Christ does not stand on the same plane as ideologies—neither those of immanence, which hold that God dwells in all things and are tempted to divinize the powers of this world, nor those of pure transcendence, which hold that the godhead is altogether remote and unapproachable and are tempted to think the world is given over to demons. Christianity proclaims that men share salvation in Christ, not only by an historical knowledge or by reflection on the historical event of salvation—which would smack of ideology—but by a communion which rises above intellectual apperception, a living together in the ever-present Church of Christ, without any philosophy being presupposed.

Unlike philosophic systems of thought and ideologies, belief in God through Jesus Christ does not take a purely negative attitude toward other religious traditions of mankind, even though its mission is to be a sign for the religions of the nations. It embraces those forms of faith which existed before and exist along with it as unconscious participations in the pardoning and divinizing grace of Christ. Thus faith in God under the auspices of Jesus

Christ is something different from systems of thought, something different from the religions of the world: it completes and transcends the ways of seeking God which we find in redemptive history, by surrender to uncontrollable mystery. As Gertrud von le Fort states in *Hymns to the Church*:

In my arms I still have flowers from the wilderness,
in my hair I still have dew
from the valleys of man's early morning. . . .
Behold, in me kneel nations that passed away long
  since,
and from out my soul how many heathen
shine forth towards the Eternal! . . .
I am the road of all their roads:
on me the millennia make their way to God.

VII

Healing and Salvation
through Faith

THE New Testament relates many miraculous cures worked by Jesus and the apostles, and often the cure is expressly made conditional on faith: "All things are possible to him who believes" (Mk. 9, 23). "Great is your faith. Be it done for you as you desire" (Mt. 15, 28). "Your faith has made you well" (Lk. 17, 19). "According to your faith be it done to you" (Mt. 9, 29). These texts clearly indicate the connection between faith and the cure of sickness.

What shall we say of the healing power of faith? People's views on this matter widely diverge, even among those who consider themselves Christians. They range from the view that faith has no more to do with healing than any other kind of suggestion, to "Christian Science" where faith, in its power to heal, has in effect become the substance of doctrine. Therefore, let us look for an answer to this difficult question which comes from faith as a whole.

In the first place, Christian faith is not indifferent to sickness, as though it were something of no importance in Christian existence. Faith sheds light on sickness and fits

it into human existence at large. Sickness as concretely
undergone by the individual is not necessarily a consequence of his sin. Jesus expressly rejects the principle that
it must be (Jn. 9, 2f.), although in other cases he does
see a connection (Mk. 2, 5; Jn. 5, 14). Thus, in effect, he
has disallowed in advance the tendency which certain
schools of medical thought have to treat all sickness, or
most, as a mere manifestation of psychic conflict or even of
guilt at the core of the person. No doubt there *are* such
cases, but not every case of sickness points to personal
guilt in the individual who is sick.

Sickness, therefore, as it is actually experienced, may
bear something of each character, the psychical and the
bodily, and thus it becomes a riddle to which no complete
solution can be found. Accordingly, faith will primarily
see in sickness what marks man's being in general: man
lives in the context of nature and at the same time is free
in an ultimate, indefinable mingling of necessity and
freedom which lies open to no eye but God's alone, who
"knows the heart" (1 Kgs. 8, 39 and *passim*).

Moreover, faith knows that all sickness, even that
which the individual incurs by no personal fault and
bears with a holy endurance, is a different thing in man
from what it is in an animal, that it is in part a manifestation of general human sinfulness. By the law of nature,
biological sickness and biological death are the inheritance
of man, who probably originated (at least in the biological
sense) in pre-human forms of life. "Adam" means "man"
—not without "Eve," for Hebrew tradition and St. Paul
look on man as representing the oneness of the two (Rom.
5, 12ff.; 1 Cor. 15, 21f. 45-49). So what is meant is not
an "inheriting" of sin but rather a general diffusion of
sin all over the human world, a loss of fellowship with
God, of "eternal life" (Rom. 5, 21), whence Christ, who

brings mankind redemption, appears as the "new Adam."
If biological sickness is mainly the concern of the medical
profession, the physical cures which Jesus effects in his
"goodness and compassion" are put to work for his real
mission, the cure of spiritual sickness and spiritual death.
Jesus is the "physician," the Savior; he saves men for
sonship of God and for eternal life. His miraculous cures
are for those who "have eyes to see"; they are "signs" of
their real purpose—"Thy sins are forgiven thee." And in
order to take this sickness away he sacrificed himself
as "a lamb for many" ("God's servant for many"). Thus
his envoys are "physicians of the soul," as the Fathers
say, particularly the Eastern Fathers.

First and foremost, faith sees in sickness that which
marks the life of the whole man: sickness is part of that
constant dying in which man lives and which reaches its
climax and its term in death. Death is not only "the wages
of sin" but also the evil which was the object of God's
saving work in Jesus Christ. He delivered himself up
"for many" (Mt. 20, 28; cf. 1 Tim. 2, 6)—that is, for all.
And so, even undergoing sickness becomes meaningful
in a man's life. When sickness is endured in surrender to
the will of God, it trains us in faith for "dying with
Christ" who died "once for all" for sinners (Rom. 6, 10).

In a doctor's eyes all illnesses are variations on a theme:
mortality. In a geologist's eyes the top layer of the earth's
crust is a graveyard of bygone life—vegetable, animal and
human. Faith considers all illnesses which the sufferer
accepts as "angels in disguise, lifting him from step to
step" (Reinhold Schneider), and the Church in her
wisdom begins Lent, on Ash Wednesday, by making a
cross in ashes on the forehead of the faithful: "Remember,
O man, that thou art dust and to dust thou shalt return."

Faith, in Scripture and the Church's liturgy, is obviously more than a mere intellectual assent to certain propositions; it is the trustful acceptance of God's love for man. The effect of this salvific faith is the forgiveness of sins, growth in love so "that we should walk in good works" (Eph. 2, 10), and patient endurance of suffering in general and of sickness in particular. Here faith does not abolish the uncontrollability of our lot but does overcome it. For a Christian, fate means the good pleasure of God who "is love" (1 Jn. 4, 8).

Against this background we can understand the saving power of faith. Faith is always a saving power—indeed the fundamental saving power in the whole of Christian life. "Salvation by faith" is a major theme of the Letter to the Romans. And for sufferers, in particular, "in the cross is salvation," because the God-Man, "by whom all things exist, in bringing many sons to glory," was made "perfect through suffering" (Heb. 2, 10). All suffering and all sickness, which seem to the profane eye a decay of life, become for the believer a summons and an acceptance and therefore a spiritual conquest of suffering, sickness and death. Thus suffering grows akin to love and accordingly embraces everything in God's world—except sin, the negation of his love. But suffering is no sin and dying is no sin, but a natural law of earthly life, the universal and inescapable evil that becomes sanctified and transfigured for Christians just as it was for Christ: "He who believes in me, though he die, yet shall he live" (Jn. 11, 25). In trusting obedience to God's will, the approach of death becomes a maturing of surrender into the eternal life of God; it becomes true life that perfects itself without end (Jn. 11, 25; 1 Tim. 6, 19).

Whether this religious point of view alters the outward manifestation of sickness with which medicine generally concerns itself is a minor question. A sick man

who wanted nothing else but that health which concerns
the doctor professionally, a sick man who simply demanded to be well again, who endured death, unbelieving,
only under protest and as something wholly absurd, who
would not so much as consider the possibility that through
death the author of life might be offering him a higher
form of life, even an "eternal life"—that man would not
understand either how different life is from "life" and
death from "death." The Apocalypse speaks of the "first"
death and the "second" death (Apoc. 2, 11; 20, 6) in the
damnation, in the next world, of the faithless and the
loveless. By contrast the saving power of faith displays
itself above all by leaving no room for the unbelieving
sick man's protest against "senseless death." It subsumes
the first stirring of nature into a second movement by the
readiness to turn our theoretical knowledge of the law of
death into a personal acceptance of God's will. The
"pioneer of faith" (Heb. 12, 2) says: "Father, if thou art
willing, remove this cup from me; nevertheless not my
will, but thine, be done." By God's saving gift to us, by
faith that we ourselves exercise, death is not an unmiti-
gated evil. Thus St. Francis was able to hail death as
his "brother":

> Laudato si, mi Signore,
> per sora nostra morte corporale,
> de la quale nullu homo
> vivente po skappare . . .
> Beati quelli ke troverà
> ne le Tue sanctissime voluntati!

"Be thou praised, Lord, by our brother, bodily death,
whom no living man escapes. . . . Blessed are those whom
he finds at one with thy most holy will!"

Many things cannot be "explained." A purely psychological explanation of particular cures (at Lourdes, for instance) smacks of evasion, especially as the power of faith is also an element that enters into psychology. Nor can the scientist calculate what nature and grace are capable of, what the power of grace may do when nature lies helpless. Peace, serenity, devotion, confidence—such feelings and states of mind themselves display the widest variety; they extend to every psychosomatic cell and member, to the whole man, from the most elemental psychosomatic mechanisms to that depth (or summit) of the spiritual person where natural desire and the power of faith intermingle, where something happens in the "spark of the soul" (as the ancients used to say) which neither doctors nor psychologists nor theologians nor Karl Marx nor the pope can "explain."

Miracles? A Christian believes in the miracle of God's eternal love in the historical incarnation of God and against that background in the miracle of Christ's resurrection as the token of our resurrection (1 Cor. 15). That miracle offers no scientific explanation of sickness and death but sheds light on the mystery of life and death. Cures ancient or modern are not explicable by pure psychology. It is no explanation to say: "Faith produces serenity of mind and confidence." Such psychological processes favor healing, but something is involved in faith that eludes complete analysis. Even the most experienced psychologist or physician will not be able to explain all cures scientifically, ruling out the decisive force of a "great faith" (Mt. 15, 28), especially inasmuch as Jesus himself associates faith with miraculous cures. There is no need to talk of the laws of nature being suspended if one admits the fact of miraculous cures, because at a propitious moment the levels of psychical life which have been disordered may so fit back together that organic laws yield to spiritual ones. Because faith embraces the whole man, therefore, and insofar as it does, faith has a saving power and a healing power. When faith is seized by the power of grace and entrusts everything, especially a man's own fate, to the absolute good pleasure of God, then by his might it can do incredible things.

VIII

Faith Today

W HAT we must have today is a brotherly faith, which means a humble faith. Faith becomes genuine not when we simply congratulate ourselves on having it, but when we identify ourselves with others who find it a struggle to believe and who ask what faith really means.

A brotherly faith also means that we do not presume to witness to anything but what we ourselves live, in pain and prayer, or at least try to. Theology is good—but how minor all theological acumen is compared with that interior strength of mind and heart which decides ultimate matters of faith, and here clerics and people trained in theology have no advantage over "laymen."

Brotherly faith, humble faith, also concerns those who think they do not believe and those who really do not believe. No sharp line can be drawn between the two groups.

We believe within the spiritual climate of our time. Spiritual life is necessarily many-sided; it draws sustenance from many sources, not from actual revelation alone. Therefore it involves a variety of spiritual knowledge and impulses even in the Christian, and faces the individual in his personal freedom with decision about the mystery of God. Here the altered world picture, stressing as it does the exaltation of God above the world (see above), may make faith particularly anguishing, for it is a world where God's governance seems almost completely hidden behind the laws of nature. Faith must not deny this situation in which we find ourselves today. We know that we are caught in a web of earthly laws. This experience makes our faith sober and unpretentious. The word "God" does not come so readily to our lips; we do not presume to behave as though we had comprehended the mystery of God. Unbelievers, as they are called, seem brothers to us so long as they are serious-minded men. At least we cannot despise them. But there is no question of any conflict between faith and experience of the world.

No doubt faith today is in jeopardy, as it always has been, but it remains the task and the hallmark of Christian existence in the world, and once we perceive this fact and take it in, then by God's grace everything else is "added unto" us. A man who believes finds himself especially threatened today by earthly experience, but faith remains the foundation of all our life.

The individual priest and theologian will admit that in this age of scientific and technological thinking he cannot of himself bring forward a positive, direct, objectively satisfying vindication of Christian revelation and belief in God. Now admitting our real jeopardy is no adequate cure for an ailing faith, but it is the necessary beginning of a cure. God's strength is masterful precisely in our weakness. The real threat from concrete intellectual difficulties—whether presented by natural science, exegesis or the history of religions—is not so much to individual doctrines as to faith in general, given the variety of philosophies which men profess, the strains that exist between the formularies of faith and its reality, the apparently senseless cruelties of history, the impotence of the spirit when faced by the might of the flesh and the constant dominion of violence over defenseless truth. We must indeed confess that faith stands in jeopardy.

And precisely this acute situation brings it home to man that the world is not God and he is not God—that neither the world nor man has any native splendor which can be peacefully enjoyed. Now in this way, and in no other, man learns that God is *God,* that incomprehensible mystery to which complete surrender is the grace of faith. And in this grace the believer experiences God's forgiving, self-communicating intimacy.

The faith of our day is an altogether simple faith. Contemporary man thinks of a God essentially exalted above all things, absolute, incomprehensible. He balks at the idea that God has, as it were, taught us an arbitrary set of propositions, drawn from the infinite treasure of his knowledge, without its being at all clear how knowing and accepting them bears on the living of human life. In the Christian religion, when all is said and done, there are only three absolute mysteries: that of the triune God, that of God's incarnation in Jesus Christ, and that of the grace which divinizes us. And these three are most intimately connected, together forming a single salvation, for each one who receives the message must answer for himself, standing before the mystery of God, whose message, coming from without, is received in an experience of inward grace, unto a forgiving and loving intimacy with God through sharing his life.

Faith, for a Christian, means opening himself to the mystery of the unutterably loving God, not in words alone

but in the existential following of Christ. For he lived the
fellowship of God and man in matchless perfection and
is therefore called the "pioneer and perfecter of faith"
(Heb. 12, 2). At the same time, faith means a deeper
penetration of the content of faith, not in the sense of
getting the intellectual meat out of this or that proposition
but in the sense of getting our values into order and per-
spective. For example, it is far from easy to know what
prayer is and how it happens. Is it mere unconscious auto-
suggestion? One might be inclined to think so until one
realizes that the word "Father" is no childish, subjective
notion gigantically overblown in an attempt to cope with
life, but that God in his immeasurable love empowers
me, gives me the capacity and the freedom, to respond to
his love with reverent thanks, trusting him and beseeching
him. The labors and lessons that this involves are an
essential part of personal growth in faith, compared with
which mere intellectual deductions from theology as to
how modern man can lead a Christian life pale into rela-
tive insignificance.

I suppose everyone knows that all human ideas and
statements about God are analogical (like and unlike)
in character, even Christians with little education. But
how far they embody this knowledge in concrete piety is
another matter. The mind of a child—certainly a lovely
thing—is very apt to overlook the fact that human ideas
and images of God are more unlike God than like him.
For God is just that—God, not a semi-human being. Perhaps most atheists in the West only take offense at and
have only become atheists over the concept of a God who
seemed to be the top part, the keystone, of the world.
God lets men go their ways in freedom; he is and always
will be the unutterable mystery, beyond all that we can

imagine. We must admit that a great many Christians, even priests, often speak unwittingly of God as though he had appeared to them in human form. Certainly God became man in Jesus Christ, who possesses human nature, and in this human nature of the Lord has become like us, apart from sin (Heb. 2, 17; 4, 15). But God in his eternal nature has not become part of the world; his mystery outstrips all concepts, even those which are true as far as they go.

Let us add another point, an important one. The way Christian faith is explained often fails to make it clear that we are dealing ultimately not with concepts and propositions about the mystery of God, but with the living encounter between the inner man and God, when God communicates himself to man and man accepts him by God's grace. This self-communication of God is not confined within the limits of the visible Church; her members live in the midst of others who are not mere "pagans," people afar off from God. Everywhere it is an open question whether in the living of their lives men will accept the mystery above them in trustful love or sinfully squander themselves in the finitude of their own being.

On considering these things, we become aware that as Christians we may not look on our fellow men as mere "pagans," as though there were nothing Christian about them at all and we had to sow the first seeds of divine truth in their hearts with our stammering—with words that are forever inadequate. We may and should assume that we are dealing with people who are already pardoned but have not yet found themselves to the extent of explicitly belonging to the community of Christian believers.

This assumption will have its effect on our attitude. It makes our faith more generous, more patient, more confident. At first sight we are God's "little flock," living among ferocious wolves. There are Christians in that position, of course, but our position is somewhat different. We live among little lambs of Christ, many of whom have gone astray and not yet found their way home, or who outwardly look like wolves but inwardly, by God's grace, have perhaps turned into gentle little lambs of God, even though they do not know it.

Faith of this kind allows God to be greater than our mind, our heart and our concept of the Church, since the very faith of the Church says that God is greater than anything else. Greater means mightier, more gracious, more victorious, in control even of those roads which we never find, having mercy even where we cannot say one explicit word of pardon. A man with such faith is patient, knowing that what seems to us to be God's hesitancy is the proof of his longanimity and grace. A man with such faith is not ashamed of the Gospel. Aware of God's redemptive will to pardon men, at once modestly and boldly (out of thanksgiving for his own vocation) he finds occasion to trust hidden grace in those who seem to be far off from God's kingdom and may be nearer than we think.

What we ourselves are, we have received by God's free grace; from the faith of our fathers and mothers we have received faith for our own life, the faith that was from the beginning and grew more and more conscious of itself, in the course of mankind's history, as the history of salvation, until God's Word and man's hearkening, promise and fulfillment, fused, matchlessly one, in Jesus Christ. The faith with which the Church concerns herself is quite simple. It says the one, tremendous thing that is all we can live by: that God, the eternal mystery, gives himself to us. Faith, of course, is always given to us in such a way that we must keep praying for it anew in the struggles of life, for it remains God's grace.

IX

Can God Be Experienced?

W HAT we mean to discuss now is not a pious feeling, some holiday mood or religious uplift with a hymn, perhaps, in the background, but an objective, grace-given experience of God comparable in some respects to what Jesus experienced in his human nature by reason of God's incarnation when he, the eternal Word made flesh, the eternal Son in the triune godhead, as man like us in all things excepting sin (Heb. 2, 17; 4, 15), became aware of his deep bond with the Father at the same moment when his human consciousness first awoke, so that as a growing boy he could say quite naturally: "Did you not know that I must be in my Father's house?" and when the time had come went forth, "full of the Holy Spirit . . . to preach Good News to the poor" (Lk. 4, 18; cf. Mt. 12, 18).

Is there in the experience of the pardoned anything comparable with this unique thing, "natural" to the God-Man? Can we experience God's grace at all in this life? Would that not be to destroy grace, the bright-dark cloud which envelops us as long as we are pilgrims here on earth? The mystics say that there is experience of God, and they would seal the truth of what they say with their

lifeblood. They claim to have actually experienced God
and his grace. But there is no discussing mystical experiences if one does not have them—and a man who has them
may not talk about them unless he is commanded outright
to do so. Nevertheless, perhaps there are degrees in experience of God's grace, of which the lowest ones can be
reached even by people like us.

First let us ask: Have you ever experienced the
spiritual element in man? And the answer may be: Yes,
I have had this experience and have it every day. I think,
I decide, I love, I rejoice over values like knowledge and
art. So I know what spirit is. Now the matter is not so
simple. For in the examples that have been cited "spirit"
is only a kind of extra benefit from earthly life which
makes it beautiful and in some way significant. But this
does not mean that we are experiencing anything at all
of the transcendent divine Spirit. Where are we to find
experience of that Spirit who is anything but an intrinsic
element of natural life? Only a modest word or two can
be said about this, perhaps by mentioning cases where
a spiritual experience of God seems credible.

Have we ever kept silent, despite the urge to defend
ourselves, when we were being unfairly treated? Have we
ever forgiven another although we gained nothing by it
and our forgiveness was accepted as quite natural? Have
we ever made a sacrifice without receiving any thanks or
acknowledgment, without even feeling any inward satis-
faction? Have we ever decided to do a thing simply for
the sake of conscience, knowing that we must bear sole
responsibility for our decision without being able to explain it to anyone? Have we ever tried to act purely for
love of God when no warmth sustained us, when our act
seemed a leap in the dark, simply nonsensical? Were we
ever good to someone without expecting a trace of grati-

tude and without the comfortable feeling of having been "unselfish"?

If we can find such experiences in our life, then we have had that very experience of the Spirit which we are after here—the experience of the Eternal, the experience that the Spirit is something more than and different from a part of this world, the experience that happiness in this world is not the whole point of existence, the experience of trust as we sink into darkness, the experience of a faith for which this world provides no reason. In this context we can understand what secret passion burns in the real men of the Spirit and in the saints. Penetrated though they be with the "Lord, I am not worthy," they are bent on having this experience. At their vitals gnaws a fear of sticking in this world, and so they crave a pledge that they have already begun to live in the Spirit. Whereas for ordinary men such experiences are only unpleasant interruptions of normal life which cannot quite be avoided, the men of the Spirit and the saints find in them a taste of the pure Spirit—hence their strange life, their poverty, their cult of humility, their longing "to depart and be with Christ" (cf. Phil. 1, 23; 3, 12ff.). They well know that grace can bless even the reasonable doings of everyday life; they know that on earth we are not angels and are not meant to be. But by faith they know that man as a spirit must really live on the frontier between the world and God, between time and eternity. And by their messages to this person or that, they try to prove to themselves that the Spirit in them is something other than a means of living earthly life well.

Now if we have *this* experience of the Spirit—by accepting it—then we who live in faith have in fact experienced the supernatural, perhaps without quite realizing it. And we are forbidden to turn back and gaze full on the super-

natural. But we know that if we abandon ourselves to
this experience of the Spirit, if all that can be touched and
enjoyed melts away, if everything earthly ceases to matter
—then in truth not only "spirit" but the Holy Spirit is at
work in us; then the hour of God's grace has struck. Let
us read chapters four and five of Paul's Second Letter to
the Corinthians. What seems to be the riddle, the abyss
of our human existence, the bottomless mystery of God
which imparts itself to us if we have abandoned ourselves,
no longer attempting to be our own master, is the beginning of eternal life.

No doubt we shall have to turn back again to familiar
things within reach. But by degrees we shall acquire a
taste for pure wine, for the vintage that is full of God's
Spirit—at least to the extent of not refusing the cup when
God's governance hands it to us. It is the cup of Christ.
To renounce all is to gain all; to descend is to rise; to die
is to live. A man attains to this experience of the Spirit,
of the Holy Spirit of grace, in Christ by faith. It brings
him into the life of God.

One cannot say of such experience of grace: "There
it is; I have it." One can only seek it by forgetfulness of
self; one can only find it by seeking God alone.

It is advisable to ask oneself how far one still has to
go. "While we are still in this tent, we sigh with anxiety;
not that we would be unclothed, but that we would be
further clothed, so that what is mortal may be swallowed
up by life. He who has prepared us for this very thing is
God, who has given us the Spirit as a guarantee" (2 Cor.
5, 4f.) .